Win
wind,

Nottingham Forest in February 1969

Raising a glass: Bob Paisley toasts his final league championship victory with the Reds in May 1983

MOËT
PREMIÈRE
MOËT & CHANDON

Kop idol: Kenny Dalglish watches his header go wide of the post in his '80s heyday

Kop salute: Liverpool's title winners of 1990 acknowledge the home support as they complete a lap of honour at Anfield

Contents

A Mirror publication
Marketing Manager: Fergus McKenna
Mirrorpix: David Scripps and Alex Waters
020 7293 3858

Produced by Trinity Mirror Sport Media,
PO BOX 48, Liverpool L69 3EB
0151 227 2000

Exectutive Editor: Ken Rogers
Senior Editor: Steve Hanrahan
Senior Art Editor: Rick Cooke
Senior Production Editor: Paul Dove
Compiled and written by: William Hughes and Alan Jewell
Designers: Jamie Dunmore and James Kenyon
Sub Editors: Mike Haydock and Adam Oldfield

Part of the Mirror Collection

Images: Mirrorpix, PA Photos
Printed by PCP

RACE IS ON FOR NUMBER 19

LIVERPOOL AND MANCHESTER. TWO CITIES IN THE NORTH-WEST OF ENGLAND; ONE OF THE BIGGEST RIVALRIES IN WORLD FOOTBALL. THE CLUBS FROM THE RED HALVES OF THEIR RESPECTIVE HOMES NOW HAVE 18 TITLES APIECE. WHO WILL GET TO 19 FIRST?

LIVERPOOL Football Club has won more trophies than any other English side.

For years their tally of 18 league titles seemed untouchable, but the advent of the Premier League also saw the dawn of a new era at Manchester United.

When Liverpool last won the league title in 1990, their 18th triumph took them 11 championships clear of the Old Trafford club in the game's roll of honour.

Back then, Sir Alex Ferguson was into his fourth season in charge of United and had just won his first piece of silverware in the shape of the FA Cup. He resolved to take the challenge to his Anfield rivals and set about the business of knocking them off their perch.

The truth may hurt, but much as Liverpool dominated English football throughout the 1970s and 1980s, so United have been top dog during the 1990s and 2000s.

It was at the start of the 20th century that Liverpool first registered a league title victory, in 1900/01, and United have generally been playing catch-up since.

After 1910/11 the score was 2-2 but as the 1950s dawned Liverpool had a 5-2 lead. The Busby Babes won three titles within six seasons to level things up again and from 1963/64 the sides alternated championships for four seasons and the tally remained at 7-7 until Liverpool triumphed in 1972/73.

This was the beginning of a period where Liverpool reigned supreme, winning 11 titles within 18 seasons under Shankly, Paisley, Fagan and Dalglish.

During this spell, United strove unsuccessfully to claim a single championship, a drought that became a saga in itself. At the start of every season the question would be posed: Can they finally do it? United would always be found wanting and the embarrassment was exacerbated by what the team at the other end of the East Lancashire Road was achieving.

But as Liverpool's run ended in 1990, so United came to the fore. After a near miss in 1992, they finally claimed the championship in 1993. This was the first of 11 titles in 17 seasons.

The Premier League title has so far eluded Liverpool while it has been a regular fixture in the Old Trafford trophy cabinet. Last season saw Liverpool, led by Rafa Benitez, push them harder than ever, but United

Glory days: Peter Beardsley and Craig Johnston lead the title celebrations in 1988

MIRROR SPORT

EXCLUSIVE! FREE! SUPER OFFER
FABULOUS PANINI WORLD CUP STICKERS AND ALBUM
TURN TO PAGE 25

FURY!

MARK HUGHES brushes off Ryan's challenge. Pic: ALBERT COOPER

United jeered

By BOB RUSSELL
Man U 0, Wimb'don 0

WEMBLEY-BOUND Manchester United and Wimbledon were booed off by Old Trafford's lowest League gate of the season as a furious crowd reacted to a match lacking any passion or commitment.

The 29,281 fans who anticipated a bright end-of-season contest, gave it the thumbs down – and rightly so.

United manager Alex Ferguson stated the terms of this easy-going encounter by leaving out four of next week's FA Cup final squad.

Skipper Bryan Robson, his England midfield partner Neil Webb, striker Brian McClair and Scotland goalkeeper Jim Leighton were rested for a game watched by Steve Coppell, manager of Wembley opponents Crystal Palace.

But Ferguson, who also kept winger Danny Wallace on the subs bench until the second half, must have been wondering whether he

Turn to page 31

WILL ENGLAND HAVE THE DANISH FOR BREAKFAST?
TUESDAY 15TH MAY
KICK OFF 8PM
ENGLAND v DENMARK
PRECEDED BY ENGLAND v POLAND U18 AT 6PM
TICKET PRICES
CLUB OLYMPIC £30
ADULTS (NO STANDING) £17.50 £15 £12.50 £10
FAMILY ENCLOSURE
ADULTS £12.50 £10 CHILDREN HALF PRICE
COUNTER SALES ONLY
NO BOOKING FEE
OPP. TOTT CT. RD. TUBE
Virgin megastore (01-862 0202 - INFO ONLY)
WEMBLEY BOX OFFICE
01-900 1990/1234
All major credit cards accepted
WEMBLEY UPDATE FOR EVENT DETAILS
0898 600 500
WEMBLEY VENUE OF LEGENDS

LOOK WHO'S BACK!

It's boss Kenny

LIVERPOOL fans could get a surprise addition to their championship-winning side tonight – manager Kenny Dalglish playing against Derby County.

Anfield will be awash with emotion as their heroes receive the championship trophy – Liverpool's 18th title.

By ALEC JOHNSON

But the sight of their hero back in a red shirt again among his triumphant players will cause the Kop to erupt with excitement.

It is what every Liverpool supporter wants to see, and there is tremendous support within Anfield itself for the former Scottish international to give the night that special thrill with a return performance.

The idea sprang up over the weekend when former Liverpool star Graeme Souness, now manager of Glasgow Rangers, played in their 2-0 defeat of Dunfermline to celebrate winning the Premier League.

But Dalglish's appearance would be no gimmick.

The super-fit 39-year-old Scot is only contemplating his first match in the side for nearly two years because at least five key first team men are doubtful through injury.

They are skipper Alan Hansen, Ray Houghton, Ronnie Whelan, Peter Beardsley and David Burrows.

Dalglish confirmed he could play tonight, but warned: "If it is going to disappoint someone else then it won't happen."

WORLD WAR! Turn to Pages 30, 31

9 770956 805004

King's crown: The Daily Mirror reports on Liverpool's title triumph in May 1986 when boss Kenny Dalglish scored the goal which clinched the first part of the double

Title trio: Kevin Keegan, Tommy Smith and Emlyn Hughes parade the league championship trophy around Anfield in 1973

He made the people happy: Gordon Banks holds aloft Bill Shankly's arm as they salute the Anfield fans in August 1973

held on to draw level with the Reds on 18 titles as they notched their 11th Premier League success.

The general consensus is that one of the two clubs will end 2009/10 with 19, which suggests the 2009/10 season will be something special.

The enmity that has developed between Benitez and Sir Alex Ferguson will only add spice to the contest. Expect plenty of references to 'mind games' in the months ahead.

Race for No. 19 is a celebration of Liverpool Football's Club's title successes down the years and a look ahead to the new season as the class of 09/10 look to emulate those to have brought the domestic championship to Anfield.

Using the fantastic Daily Mirror picture vault and the incredible newspaper archive, this magazine brings you rarely seen images as well as an insight into how each of the 18 championships were reported at the time.

From the first successes under the leadership of Liverpool's longest-serving manager, Tom Watson, to the Reds' final three triumphs under Kenny Dalglish, the magazine looks back at how those titles were won and salutes the key figures behind the glory days.

It also previews the 2009/10 campaign as Steven Gerrard and his team-mates seek to bring the club's 20-year wait for a title to an end by claiming championship number 19.

The race is on: let battle commence.

Toshack warrior: John Toshack beats Arsenal's Frank McLintock to the ball as Bob McNab looks on in November 1970

Above: Bob Paisley and Emlyn Hughes celebrate clinching Liverpool's 10th title in 1977

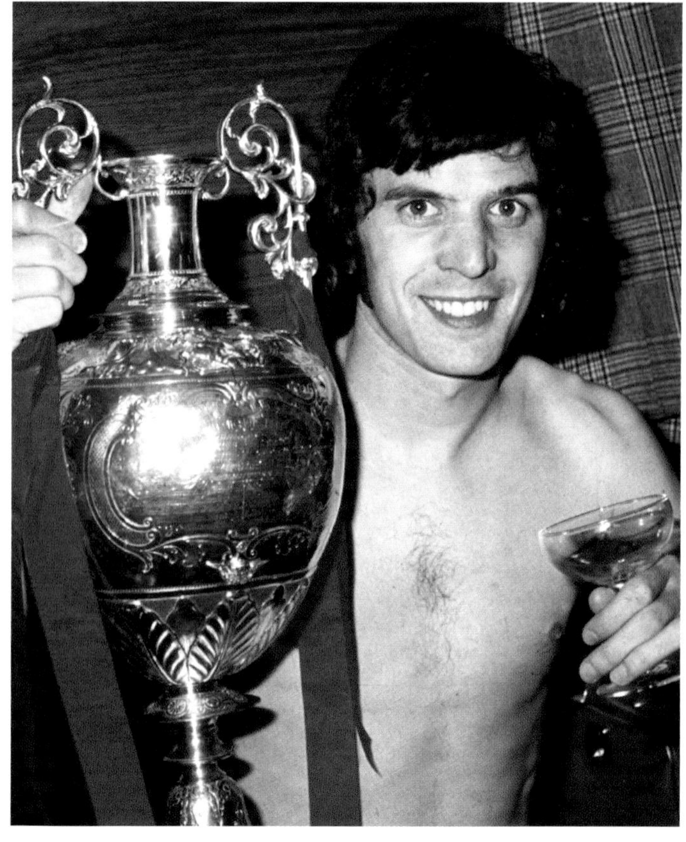

Right: Peter Cormack toasts championship success in 1973

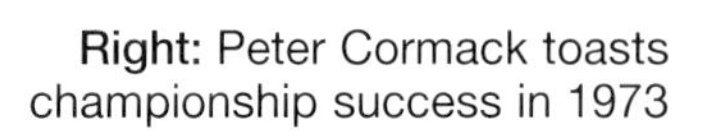

Surprise, surprise: Cilla Black drops in at Melwood to see Bill Shankly take charge of training

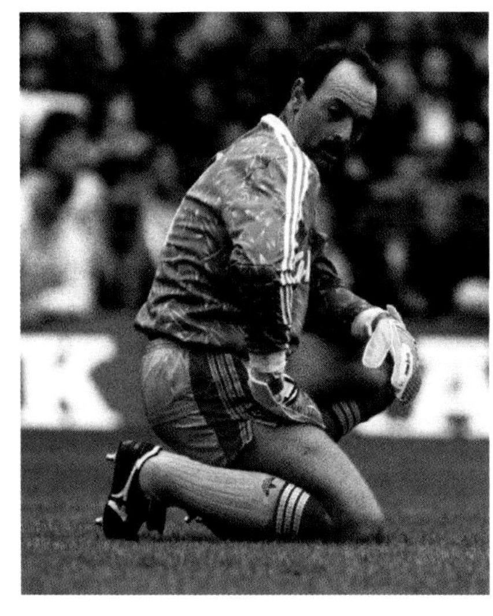

Fans' favourite: Bruce Grobbelaar played a role in the glory years

Future King: Kenny Dalglish in his youth

LIVERPOOL V MANCHESTER UNITED DECADE BY DECADE

1900-1910

1900/01:	**Liverpool league champions**
1905/06:	**Liverpool league champions**
1907/08:	Manchester United league champions
1908:	Manchester United Charity Shield winners
1908/09:	Manchester United FA Cup winners

1910-1920

1910/11:	Manchester United league champions
1911:	Manchester United Charity Shield winners

1910-1920

1921/22:	**Liverpool league champions**
1922/23:	**Liverpool league champions**

1930-1940

	No major trophies won by either side

1940-1950

1946/47:	**Liverpool league champions**
1947/48:	Manchester United FA Cup winners

1950-1960

1951/52:	Manchester United league champions
1952:	Manchester United Charity Shield winners
1955/56:	Manchester United league champions
1956:	Manchester United Charity Shield winners
1956/57:	Manchester United league champions
1957:	Manchester United Charity Shield winners

1960-1970

1962/63:	Manchester United FA Cup winners
1963/64:	**Liverpool league champions**
1964:	**Liverpool Charity Shield shared**
1964/65:	Manchester United league champions
	Liverpool FA Cup winners
1965:	**Liverpool and Manchester United share Charity Shield**
1965/66:	**Liverpool league champions**
1966:	**Liverpool Charity Shield winners**
1966/67:	Manchester United league champions
1967:	Manchester United Charity Shield shared
1967/68:	Manchester United European Cup winners

1970-1980

1972/73:	**Liverpool league champions**
	Liverpool UEFA Cup winners
1973/74:	**Liverpool FA Cup winners**
1974:	**Liverpool Charity Shield winners**
1975/76:	**Liverpool league champions**
	Liverpool UEFA Cup winners
1976:	**Liverpool Charity Shield winners**
1976/77:	**Liverpool league champions**
	Liverpool European Cup winners
	Manchester United FA Cup winners
1977:	**Liverpool and Manchester United share Charity Shield**
1977/78:	**Liverpool European Cup winners**
	Liverpool European Super Cup winners
1978/79:	**Liverpool league champions**
1979:	**Liverpool Charity Shield winners**
1979/80:	**Liverpool league champions**

1980-1990

1980:	**Liverpool Charity Shield winners**
1980/81:	**Liverpool European Cup winners**
	Liverpool League Cup winners
1981/82:	**Liverpool league champions**
	Liverpool League Cup winners
1982:	**Liverpool Charity Shield winners**
1982/83:	**Liverpool league champions**
	Manchester United FA Cup winners
	Liverpool League Cup winners
1983:	Manchester United Charity Shield winners
1983/84:	**Liverpool league champions**
	Liverpool European Cup winners
	Liverpool League Cup winners
1984/85:	Manchester United FA Cup winners
1985/86:	**Liverpool league champions**
	Liverpool FA Cup winners
1986:	**Liverpool Charity Shield shared**
1987/88:	**Liverpool league champions**
1988:	**Liverpool Charity Shield winners**
1988/89:	**Liverpool FA Cup winners**
1989:	**Liverpool Charity Shield winners**
1989/90:	**Liverpool league champions**
	Manchester United FA Cup winners

1990-2000

1990:	**Liverpool and Manchester United share Charity Shield**
1990/91:	Manchester United European Cup Winners' Cup winners
1991/92:	**Liverpool FA Cup winners**
	Manchester United League Cup winners
	Manchester United European Super Cup winners
1992/93:	Manchester United league champions
1993:	Manchester United Charity Shield winners
1993/94:	Manchester United league champions
	Manchester United FA Cup winners
1994:	Manchester United Charity Shield winners
1994/95:	**Liverpool League Cup winners**
1995/96:	Manchester United league champions
	Manchester United FA Cup winners
1996:	Manchester United Charity Shield winners
1996/97:	Manchester United league champions
1997:	Manchester United Charity Shield winners
1998/99:	Manchester United league champions
	Manchester United European Cup winners
	Manchester United FA Cup winners
1999/00:	Manchester United league champions
	Manchester United Intercontinental Cup winners

2000-2009

2000/01:	Manchester United league champions
	Liverpool UEFA Cup winners
	Liverpool FA Cup winners
	Liverpool League Cup winners
2001:	**Liverpool Charity Shield winners**
2001/02:	**Liverpool European Super Cup winners**
2002/03:	Manchester United league champions
	Liverpool League Cup winners
2003:	Manchester United Community Shield winners
2003/04:	Manchester United FA Cup winners
2004/05:	**Liverpool European Cup winners**
2005/06:	**Liverpool European Super Cup winners**
	Manchester United League Cup winners
2006:	**Liverpool Community Shield winners**
2006/07:	Manchester United league champions
2007:	Manchester United Community Shield winners
2007/08:	Manchester United league champions
	Manchester United European Cup winners
2008:	Manchester United Community Shield winners
2008/09:	Manchester United league champions
	Manchester United Club World Championship winners

THE EARLY YEARS

NINE YEARS AFTER THE SPLIT FROM EVERTON, LIVERPOOL FOOTBALL CLUB WON THEIR FIRST LEAGUE CHAMPIONSHIP. MANY MORE WOULD FOLLOW. THE SUCCESS OF THE 1900/01 TEAM WAS THE FIRST OF FOUR TITLES SECURED IN THE YEARS BEFORE THE SECOND WORLD WAR

Great Scott: Goalkeeper Elisha Scott, seen here in action against Aston Villa in September 1933, was a crowd favourite at Anfield

PAVING THE WAY FOR A WINNING PEDIGREE

AFTER winning the Lancashire League in their first season, Liverpool successfully applied to join the Second Division the following season.

They won the league and were promoted to the First Division, but finished their first season in the top-flight bottom of the pile.

Liverpool learned the lessons quickly and bounced back by winning the Second Division again for the second time in three seasons.

Their next spell in the top division would prove to be more successful.

With Tom Watson overseeing team affairs, the Reds secured their first championship in 1900/01 and were champions again in 1905/06.

Watson would stay in his role for 19 years, making him Liverpool's longest-serving manager to date.

He guided his club to the FA Cup final for the first time in 1914 but Liverpool were edged out 1-0 by Burnley in the final at Crystal Palace.

The Reds' next taste of glory came in the 1920s as they secured back-to-back championships in 1921/22 and 1922/23.

They had to wait another 24 years before they would lift the trophy again but by now a strong top-flight pedigree had been established.

FINAL TABLE 1900/01

		Pld	W	D	L	F	A	GA	Pts
1	**Liverpool**	**34**	**19**	**7**	**8**	**59**	**35**	**1.69**	**45**
2	Sunderland	34	15	13	6	57	26	2.19	43
3	Notts County	34	18	4	12	54	46	1.17	40
4	Nottingham Forest	34	16	7	11	53	36	1.47	39
5	Bury	34	16	7	11	53	37	1.43	39
6	Newcastle United	34	14	10	10	42	37	1.14	38
7	Everton	34	16	5	13	55	42	1.31	37
8	Sheffield Wednesday	34	13	10	11	52	42	1.24	36
9	Blackburn Rovers	34	12	9	13	39	47	0.83	33
10	Bolton Wanderers	34	13	7	14	39	55	0.71	33
11	Manchester City	34	13	6	15	48	58	0.83	32
12	Derby County	34	12	7	15	55	42	1.31	31
13	Wolves	34	9	13	12	39	55	0.71	31
14	Sheffield United	34	12	7	15	35	52	0.67	31
15	Aston Villa	34	10	10	14	45	51	0.88	30
16	Stoke City	34	11	5	18	46	57	0.81	27
17	Preston North End	34	9	7	18	49	75	0.65	25
18	West Bromwich Albion	34	7	8	19	35	62	0.56	22

Daily Mirror, April 17, 1906

BANK HOLIDAY FOOTBALL RESULTS.

Liverpool are the new League champions. The rule was made absolute yesterday. To have lost the first honours Liverpool had to be twice beaten and Preston North End had to wi: their last three games. But Preston North End put themselves absolutely out of the running at Roker Park, and were well beaten by Sunderland. The North Enders have played pluckily and well. They were unfortunate at some critical parts of the season in being deprived of the services of certain of their leading players; but, of course, the same comment holds good in the case of the new champions.

* * *

It was just as well that Liverpool had made themselves secure, for yesterday they went under to Bolton Wanderers. The Liverpool men are to be heartily congratulated on their feat of winning the Second and First League championships in successive years, and also getting into the semi-final of the Cup this season. And Liverpool began the season very badly at Plumstead by losing the match to the Arsenal and having Parkinson's wrist broken. Parkinson is a superb forward, and has done great work for his side since his recovery. Even yesterday he scored the two goals credited to Liverpool.

Loyal servant: Left-half Tom Bromilow played more than 300 games for the Reds between 1919 and 1930

FINAL TABLE 1905/06

		Pld	W	D	L	F	A	GA	Pts
1	**Liverpool**	**38**	**23**	**5**	**10**	**79**	**46**	**1.72**	**51**
2	Preston North End	38	17	13	8	54	39	1.39	47
3	Sheffield Wednesday	38	18	8	12	63	52	1.21	44
4	Newcastle United	38	18	7	13	74	48	1.54	43
5	Manchester City	38	19	5	14	73	54	1.35	43
6	Bolton Wanderers	38	17	7	14	81	67	1.21	41
7	Birmingham City	38	17	7	14	65	9	1.10	41
8	Aston Villa	38	17	6	15	72	56	1.29	40
9	Blackburn Rovers	38	16	8	14	54	52	1.04	40
10	Stoke City	38	16	7	15	54	55	0.98	39
11	Everton	38	15	7	16	70	66	1.06	37
12	Arsenal	38	15	7	16	62	64	0.97	37
13	Sheffield United	38	15	6	17	57	62	0.92	36
14	Sunderland	38	15	5	18	61	70	0.87	35
15	Derby County	38	14	7	17	39	58	0.67	35
16	Notts County	38	11	12	15	55	71	0.78	34
17	Bury	38	11	10	17	57	74	0.77	32
18	Middlesbrough	38	10	11	17	56	71	0.79	31
19	Nottingham Forest	38	13	5	20	58	79	0.73	31
20	Wolves	38	8	7	23	58	99	0.59	23

LEAGUE WINNERS.

Liverpool and Bristol—Chelsea's Fight—Teams To Go Down.

BY THROSTLE.

Hearty congratulations to Liverpool on account of their winning the League championship. The Anfield club has established a record, for in successive seasons they have won the Second and First Division championships. This season's record is the more wonderful, for, despite losing their opening four matches, the men from the seaport city have since played so consistently as to give the remaining clubs what practically amounted to a month's start.

* * *

The performance is little short of wonderful, and the talented team wearing the Liverpool colours certainly deserve the honour which has come their way.

* * *

Bristol City are champions of the Second Division, and equally certain of promotion are Manchester United. Chelsea hunted the Clayton team pretty close for second place, but the inability to defeat the Mancunians at Stamford Bridge, and a similar failure at Glossop, quite put the London club out of the running.

* * *

All the same, Chelsea have done extraordinarily well, and next year should see them in first class company. The problem as to which club should descend with Wolverhampton Wanderers to the Second Division from the First is still unanswered. Middlesbrough's victory over Sunderland and the rout of Bury at Gigg lane by Newcastle United was a bad omen for the Lancashire team. The sensational win of the ex-Cupholders at Birmingham, however, once more gives them a chance of escaping degradation, and it will be a desperately near thing as to whether the Lancastrians or Middlesbrough figure in the Second Division next season. Certainly general sympathy lies with Bury as the financially poorer club.

* * *

I hear on the best authority that the Manchester City-Meredith case is likely to lead to something sensational. Mutual recriminations have formed the basis upon which the commission will act. It is freely acknowledged that the rules have been broken, and I can only say that even if the verdict be adverse to everybody concerned, those who suffer will be unfortunate, inasmuch as they will have been found out, whereas many who transgress escape. It is a great pity that the game cannot be carried on without these repeated transgressions of the laws.

* o *

To-morrow will see the event of the year in the final of the English Cup, between Newcastle United and Everton. It is not within my province to go over the ground covered by my colleagues on the *Daily Mirror*, but I may be allowed to express the opinion that Newcastle will win.

LIVERPOOL EASY CHAMPIONS.

By S. B. ASHWORTH (League International).

Although all interest in football must have been concentrated in the great event at the Palace, one cannot forget the stern struggle raging at the foot of the League ladder, where Bury and Middlesbrough are fighting to the bitter end, and Notts Forest have "nowt" to throw away, as they say in Lancashire. Bury gave their goal average a big lift by trouncing Blackburn Rovers by five clear goals, and they worked with tremendous energy right through the piece.

Middlesbrough had not quite such a soft thing on with the Arsenal as their supporters fondly hoped, and but for an accident to Gray early on there is no telling what might have happened. However, thanks to a couple of goals by the matchless Common, they came through on the right side, and the interest in the fight against relegation is maintained right to the end of the season.

Notts Forest found Birmingham tough customers and Robinson a great keeper, so I suppose they were quite content to win, however small the margin. That surprise victory of theirs at Sunderland the other week seems worth something to them. Liverpool drew away from the "ruck" by a clever win over Sheffield United, and are winning in a common canter, instead of by the short head, as at one time seemed very probable. How proud Liverpudlians must feel, with both "The" trophies in their midst.

Perhaps the chief interest in the match at Wolverhampton was centred in the fact that a goal to Derby would bring the total of goals against the Wolves to a level century. But the Wolves had evidently made up their minds that this should not be, for they kept play at the other end to such purpose that they actually registered seven chalks, and Derby failed to improve on the "ninety-nine." When one glances at the County's lowly position, it seems incredible that they were leaders for a considerable period early in the season.

The remaining matches were of little importance. North End beat Bolton by three goals at Deepdale, the Villa just got the better of Notts County, and Manchester City trounced Sunderland at Hyde-road, before a crowd of exceptionally meagre proportions.

In Division II. Bristol won again away, and further improved their magnificent record. Their stable companions for promotion are Manchester United, whose ambitions are at last deservedly realised. The match at Chelsea meant very little to the Pensioners, but much to Gainsborough, as their fine win gives them another chance to escape the last three, the battle against which is quite as interesting as in the senior division.

CAN LIVERPOOL BEAT RECORD?

Six Points Required in Last Three Games.

INTERNATIONAL TEAM.

Liverpool are to be congratulated on winning the First League championship for the first time since 1906. Now the only thing is, can the Anfield-road team beat West Bromwich Albion's record number of points, 60, gained in 1919-20?

At present they have 55, and still have three games to play. Thus it is just possible to set up a new record.

Burnley came very near to setting up a new record last season, but by only earning one point in their last two games their total fell one short of the Albion's.

By the way, what a wonderfully consistent team Burnley have been since the war ended. They finished second to the Albion in 1920, won the championship last season, and stand a good chance of gaining runners-up medals again this season.

CONSISTENT SIDE.

Right through the season Liverpool have been consistent rather than brilliant. Of the thirty-nine games they have played, thirteen were drawn and they make curious reading. Ten of them ended 1—1 and the other three 0—0.

In sixteen matches their opponents have failed to score, and on only three occasions, apart from the goalless draws, have they themselves failed to find the net.

Of the players who have helped to win the honour eight are internationals. Scott (goal) and Lacey (forward) have represented Ireland on numerous occasions, Longworth and Lucas (backs), Bromilow (half) and Chambers (forward) have played for England, McKinley (back) and McNab (half) for Scotland, and Parry (back) for Wales.

Daily Mirror, April 19, 1922

LIVERPOOL are to be congratulated on winning the First League championship for the first time since 1906.

Now the only thing is, can the Anfield Road team beat West Bromwich Albion's record number of points, 60, gained in 1919/20?

At present they have 55, and still have three games to play. Thus it is just possible to set up a new record.

Burnley came very near to setting up a new record last season, but by only earning one point in their last two games their total fell one short of the Albion's.

By the way, what a wonderfully consistent team Burnley have been since the war ended. They finished second to the Albion in 1920 won the championship last season, and stand a good chance of gaining ruuners-up medals again this season.

CONSISTENT SIDE

Right through the season Liverpool have been consistent rather than brilliant. Of the thirty-nine games they have played, thirteen were drawn and they make curious reading. Ten of them ended 1-1 and the other three 0-0.

In sixteen matches their opponents have failed to score, and on only three occasions, apart from the goalless draws, have they themselves failed to find the net.

Of the eight players who have helped to win the homour, eight are internationals.

Scott (goal) and and Lacey (forward) have represented Ireland on numeorous occasions, Longworth and Lucas (backs), Bromilow (half) and Chambers (forward) have played for England, McKinley (back) and McNab (half) for Scotland and Parry (back) for Wales.

FOOTBALL'S FINISH.

Honours for Forest, Saints, Stoke and Stockport County.

King Football is dead: long live King Cricket. With the exception of one or two matches, the winter game, which has dragged too long, is over.

It is true we are to have the meeting of Liverpool, the League champions, and Huddersfield at Old Trafford next Wednesday for the F.A. Charity Shield, and also the final of the London Cup between the Arsenal and Crystal Palace to-day at New Cross. Those matters are outside the ordinary season of League football.

Liverpool, the champions, wound up the season in a blaze of glory by visiting West Bromwich and winning by four goals to one. That gave them a clear lead of six points over the Spurs, who finish second, a couple of points ahead of Burnley, last year's champions.

Cardiff, for a first year in the top class, have had a remarkable season; their position is the reward of clever, clean football.

HOW THEY FINISHED.

The records of the four top clubs are:—

	P.	W.	D.	L.	Goals F.	Goals A.	Pts.
Liverpool	42	22	13	7	63	36	57
Tottenham Hotspur	42	21	9	12	65	39	51
Burnley	42	22	5	15	72	54	49
Cardiff City	42	19	10	13	61	53	48

Class of 30/31: Liverpool line up for a team photograph in August 1930

FINAL TABLE 1921/22

		Pld	W	D	L	F	A	GA	Pts
1	**Liverpool**	**42**	**22**	**13**	**7**	**63**	**36**	**1.75**	**57**
2	Tottenham Hotspur	42	21	9	12	65	39	1.67	51
3	Burnley	42	22	5	15	72	54	1.33	49
4	Cardiff City	42	19	10	13	61	53	1.15	48
5	Aston Villa	42	22	3	17	74	55	1.34	47
6	Bolton Wanderers	42	20	7	15	68	59	1.15	47
7	Newcastle United	42	18	10	14	59	45	1.31	46
8	Middlesbrough	42	16	14	12	79	69	1.15	46
9	Chelsea	42	17	12	13	40	43	0.93	46
10	Manchester City	42	18	9	15	65	70	0.93	45
11	Sheffield United	42	15	10	17	59	54	1.09	40
12	Sunderland	42	16	8	18	60	62	0.97	40
13	West Brom	42	15	10	17	51	63	0.81	40
14	Huddersfield Town	42	15	9	18	53	54	0.98	39
15	Blackburn Rovers	42	13	12	17	54	57	0.95	38
16	Preston North End	42	13	12	17	42	65	0.65	38
17	Arsenal	42	15	7	20	47	56	0.84	37
18	Birmingham City	42	15	7	20	48	60	0.80	37
19	Oldham Athletic	42	13	11	18	38	50	0.76	37
20	Everton	42	12	12	18	57	55	1.04	36
21	Bradford City	42	11	10	21	48	72	0.67	32
22	Manchester United	42	8	12	22	41	73	0.56	28

Between the sticks: Sam Hardy was a regular in the Liverpool goal during the championship season of 1905/06 and went on to play for England

Last line of defence: Goalkeeper Elisha Scott, above right, played a major part in Liverpool's back-to-back title seasons of 1921/22 and 1922/23

FINAL TABLE 1922/23

		Pld	W	D	L	F	A	GA	Pts
1	**Liverpool**	**42**	**26**	**8**	**8**	**70**	**31**	**2.26**	**60**
2	Sunderland	42	22	10	10	72	54	1.33	54
3	Huddersfield Town	42	21	11	10	60	32	1.88	53
4	Newcastle United	42	18	12	12	45	37	1.22	48
5	Everton	42	20	7	15	63	59	1.07	47
6	Aston Villa	42	18	10	14	64	51	1.25	46
7	West Brom	42	17	11	14	58	49	1.18	45
8	Manchester City	42	17	11	14	50	49	1.02	45
9	Cardiff City	42	18	7	17	73	59	1.24	43
10	Sheffield United	42	16	10	16	68	64	1.06	42
11	Arsenal	42	16	10	16	61	62	0.98	42
12	Tottenham Hotspur	42	17	7	18	50	50	1.00	41
13	Bolton Wanderers	42	14	12	16	50	58	0.86	40
14	Blackburn Rovers	42	14	12	16	47	62	0.76	40
15	Burnley	42	16	6	20	58	59	0.98	38
16	Preston North End	42	13	11	18	60	64	0.94	37
17	Birmingham City	42	13	11	18	41	57	0.72	37
18	Middlesbrough	42	13	10	19	57	63	0.91	36
19	Chelsea	42	9	18	15	45	53	0.85	36
20	Nottingham Forest	42	13	8	21	41	70	0.59	34
21	Stoke City	42	10	10	22	47	67	0.70	30
22	Oldham Athletic	42	10	10	22	35	65	0.54	30

LIVERPOOL'S OPPORTUNITY.

Championship Assured If They Beat Huddersfield To-day.

Liverpool, who are now almost assured of the championship, will expect a hard match with Huddersfield, but they should win and thus place their honour beyond doubt. They are four points ahead of Sunderland, who may find Burnley too hard to beat at Turf Moor.

The Wearsiders are making several changes for this game. Mitton displaces Ferguson, Parker is ill and cannot turn out, while Prior and Wagstaffe will displace Donaldson and Paterson. The changes do not suggest increased playing strength.

Blackburn Rovers will introduce two local men, Haworth and Holland, in their team to play at Middlesbrough. They can hardly expect success, even though the home team will be without Marshall, the Scottish international, who has been placed on the transfer list.

Aston Villa will make a special effort to wipe out the defeat Everton inflicted on them at their first meeting, and they should succeed if they maintain their best home form, but the Toffee men are playing so well now that they are sure to make a grim battle for a point. One prefers the Villa's chance of success, however.

In spite of their international sacrifices, Cardiff were good enough to prevail against Sheffield United last week-end, but the placings should be reversed this afternoon. The United are a stiff proposition at Bramall-lane, and the points will probably remain with the home club.

AMATEUR CUP RETURNS TO THE SOUTH

Caledonians Beat Evesham in Extra Time.

LIVERPOOL AGAIN.

West Ham Still in the Running for the Double Event.

For the first time in their thirty-seven years of existence the London Caledonians have won the Amateur Cup. They have always been in the forefront of amateur football, but the supreme honour has hitherto been denied them. The weather on Saturday, although cold, was excellent for outdoor sports, and golf, athletics and football were in full swing, although there was an end of the season touch about the last-named game. Chief features of Saturday's sport were:—

Football.—Liverpool made themselves champions for the second year in succession, West Ham kept themselves in the running for promotion by beating Fulham, and Bristol City won the championship of the Southern Third Division.

Racing.—Favourites fared badly at Derby, where Dawn of Peace gained a clever victory in the chief handicap at the expense of Sprig of Orange.

CALIES' TRIUMPH.

Amateur Cup Brought South by the Scots.

London Caledonians won the Amateur Cup for the first time in their history on Saturday, when they beat Evesham by two goals to one, after extra time.

There was rare enthusiasm on the ground among the 14,000 spectators. Evesham had not previously been beaten this season.

Evesham, sturdy and solid, rather put the faster and cleverer Scots off their game by the whole-hearted vigour of their methods, and play was fierce rather than spectacular.

The Calies started well against the wind. Stokes and Bridges, the Evesham backs, were shaky in defence, and Sloan, catching them in two minds, dashed through and scored.

JONES EQUALISES.

This only served to put Evesham on their game. Osborne, at outside left, did some brilliant things, and the brothers Gates were hard pressed in defence. Still they held out, and Dawson, in goal, made some brilliant clearances before S. Jones headed a grand goal.

Calies seemed to falter in the second half, and but for the fact that Dawson made some fine saves from Busby and S. Jones, and the Gates' were again at their best, the "village lads" might have won.

Extra time had to be played, and the Calies seemed to get their second wind. They re-arranged their forward line, and, following smart play by Blyth, McCubbin was given an opening to win the match with a good goal.

It is not out of turn for the Calies, a club in their thirty-seventh year, to have won the Cup at last. The receipts were £1,177.

CHAMPIONS AGAIN.

Liverpool Join a Select Band of Successful League Clubs.

By taking a point from Huddersfield while Sunderland were losing at Burnley, Liverpool join a select band of clubs with the distinction of having won the League championship in successive years.

The feat has not been achieved since Sheffield Wednesday accomplished it in the seasons 1902-3 and 1903-4—just twenty years ago. Preston North End have done it; so have Sunderland. Aston Villa are the only club to do it twice, and that with only one season between the double event.

It is the fourth time the honours of the competition have been won by the Merseyside club. They are worthy winners. Easily the most consistent side in the country, they are also the best balanced. It is impossible to pick out one or two men and say: "These are the stars of the side." It is, rather, a team of stars; a team in which every man is a master of his craft.

STURGESS' VALUABLE GOAL.

The Liverpool match attracted 35,000 people to see the Anfielders gain their coveted distinction. They were kept on tenterhooks to the end, for last year's Cup-holders were a goal ahead up to five minutes from time, thanks to a goal from Mann that appeared to enter the net off one of the home defenders, leaving Elisha Scott quite unsighted.

Liverpool played with grim desperation in the closing stages to get on terms, and it was from one of Lacey's perfectly-timed centres that Sturgess headed through the goal that brought the point which meant so much to the champions. Liverpool well deserved the equaliser.

Sunderland or Huddersfield will be runners-up. The Wearsiders have the greatest chance, but they are performing below their best just now, and were beaten on Saturday at Burnley by two clear goals, Kelly and Freeman scoring the goals by which the home team won.

Frank Goddard, who meets George Cook, the Australian heavyweight, at the N.S.C.

Young, of West Ham, who has dislocated his thumb, but is likely to play in the final.

ON THE DOWN GRADE.

Stoke and Oldham to Descend to Second Division?—Chelsea Beat Finalists.

Although there is just the barest possibility of Stoke escaping their descent with Oldham to the Second Division seems inevitable.

With Stoke one has a deal of sympathy. They won promotion last season with Nottingham Forest, and ever since they have been everything but the spoilt darlings of fortune. Incidentally their companions in promotion have only just escaped the relegation bogey.

On Saturday against Newcastle, Stoke put up a fair battle, their defence struggling gamely to avert defeat, but the St. James' Park men prevailed by the only goal scored, Spencer finding the net just on the interval.

Stoke's weakness was, as it has been for the greater part of the season, in attack. Their forwards played indifferently and were seldom dangerous, though they began as if determined to make a bold bid for victory.

TAME GAME AT OLDHAM.

At Oldham the Athletic had a tame and altogether uneventful game with West Bromwich Albion, no goals being scored and neither goalkeeper being seriously troubled. The Athletic's outstanding matches are against Cardiff City, but they are five points to the bad and must go down.

Chelsea, Nottingham Forest and Birmingham have all been in the shadow of the Second Division for some weeks. At Stamford Bridge the Pensioners defeated Bolton Wanderers by three clear goals, but this was due less to the brilliance of the home team than to the fact that the Cup finalists were obviously taking no risks in face of their trying ordeal next Saturday.

Priestley opened the score for the home side with a great shot from a free kick, and Whitton put his side further ahead with a shot that went in off the crossbar. After the change of ends Wilding cleverly dribbled through, and, having lured Pym out of his goal, had an easy task in shooting into a tenantless net.

The Forest played with great dash against Manchester City and deservedly won through goals scored by Flood and Tinsley.

INTER-CLUB GOLF.

Sandy Lodge and Oxhey Share Honours—Lancashire Win First County Match.

Several interesting inter-club golf matches were decided on Saturday. At Sandy Lodge the home club met Oxhey, and after winning the singles by four to two, with two games halved, Oxhey lost the foursomes by three to one, so that honours were even on the day.

At Denham the Bar Golfing Society lost to the home club by five games to three. Henley beat East Berks on the latter's course by eleven to four, and at Forest Row, Royal Ashdown Forest defeated Crowborough by six and a half to five and a half. On the Royal St. George's course Royal Artillery beat the Household Brigade by seven to five, but the losers yesterday beat Royal Engineers by nine matches to one.

Lancashire Golf Union played their first inter-county match at St. Annes Old Links, and beat a strong Midland Counties side by nine to five.

A team representing the House of Commons visited Horsham and was defeated by the Mannings Heath Club by seventeen matches to five.

WOMEN GOLFERS BEATEN.

Men Again Win Contest at Stoke Poges—Miss Wethered Halves with Tolley.

Women golfers have yet to win a match in the series of contests between men and women, for in the annual meeting at Stoke Poges, Slough, on Saturday the men again won by ten games to four with one match halved. As in the previous meetings the women received a half, and they took their strokes at the odd holes of the round.

In the singles they did quite well, for they won four of the matches and lost five, whilst Miss Wethered, the woman champion, halved the top match with Cyril Tolley.

In the foursomes, however, every male couple was successful.

FALKINER'S 782 BREAK.

Smith Increases His Lead Despite Great Run by His Opponent.

Despite a brilliant 782 break by Falkiner during Saturday afternoon's session of his 16,000 championship billiards match with Smith at the New Holborn Hall, the latter increased his lead to over 3,000. Falkiner's break was within three of Smith's record of three years ago, and he would have secured a £50 prize had he eclipsed the ex-champion's break.

For the afternoon session Falkiner returned the splendid average of 116 for a total of 1,044, whilst Smith's figures were 74 and 668 respectively. Smith was in play with 438 unfinished, to which he added only three.

Smith compiled several century breaks during the day, and the closing scores were: Smith (in play) 8,000, Falkiner 4,963.

PROMOTION CHANCES.

West Ham's Big Effort to Enter the First League.

Although nearly all speculations in the First Division have been settled, Second Division problems are as fascinatingly uncertain as ever.

Notts County, the leaders, lost their last game but one, and are now only two points ahead of West Ham, whom they are due to meet on the last day of the season. The Hammers won all right against Fulham, but it was left to Leicester to provide the greatest surprise of the day by beating Manchester United.

Whipp scored two of the goals by which Leeds overcame Notts County and Powell got the other.

West Ham played a fine, dashing game at Upton Park, and Fulham were fortunate to escape with no more than one goal being scored against them. Reynolds did well in the Cottagers' goal, and it was after he had saved a hot shot from Brown that Thirlaway put the ball in the goalmouth for Watson to head through.

YOUNG'S INJURY.

Unfortunately for the Cup finalists, Young, their left back, dislocated his thumb in the course of the match. The injury was examined under X-rays after the game, and the opinion was expressed that he would be fit to take part in next Saturday's all-important game. Ruffell, it is gratifying to learn, is a certainty for next Saturday.

At the other end of the table Clapton Orient and Stockport County won, but Rotherham lost. The Orient are a point behind Rotherham, and may find it hard to make up leeway, but against Southampton they made no mistake. They were the better side throughout and should have won more decisively; as it was they had to be content with the lead Williams' goal gave them.

Stockport (who meet Southampton in their last two matches of the season) overcame Derby County by the odd goal of three, Wilson and Woodcock finding the net for the winners and Galloway for Derby.

BRISTOL CITY'S RETURN.

Promotion to Second League at Their First Attempt.

Bristol City have got back to the Second League at the first attempt. They defeated Watford on Saturday, and with Plymouth Argyle playing Swansea Town to a draw, all doubt was removed as to which club will finish first among the Southern Section of the Third Division.

Millwall thoroughly deserved their victory over Norwich City. Hopper, the home outside right, was much too fast for the opposing backs, and it was from his centre that Lane got the first goal within five minutes. Morris put on the second and third, and Millwall lost a fourth by a matter of seconds, Moule heading through just after the whistle had gone.

After a blank first half Southend defeated Brighton. Jenkins had the misfortune to put the ball through his own goal to give Southend both the points at issue. Swindon beat Reading 3—1, and two of their goals came from penalty kicks.

In the Northern Section the keen contest between Nelson and Bradford remains for settlement. Nelson have two matches with Walsall and an at home fixture to Wrexham. Bradford's two outstanding games are with Southport.

A penalty goal late in the game decided the match at Crewe, where the Alexandra beat Hartlepools United 2—1.

OTHER SPORT IN BRIEF.

News Items and Gossip About Men and Matters of the Moment.

Exit Port Royal.—The Lincoln failure, Port Royal, has been struck out of the City and Suburban.

Sandy Herd, who has accomplished a "hole in one" on seventeen occasions, has been appointed professional to the Moor Park G.C.

Church Lads' Brigade Sports.—St. Mary, Boltons, won the athletic championships of the Church Lads' Brigade Cadet Force (London Division).

Golf at Weybridge.—Douglas Grant (Mid-Surrey) won the annual competition for the St. George's Hill silver trophy on Saturday, with rounds of 77 and 73.

Latest Epsom Prices.—City and Suburban—9-2 Re-Echo, 6 Copyright, 15-2 Condover, 100-12 Soubriquet, 100-9 Holy Friar, 100-8 Eaglehawk (t), 100-6 Dry Toast.

Alf Bright's Easy Win.—Alf Bright, of Kingsland, gained an easy victory over Fred Sale, of Darleston, at the Ring on Saturday, the latter retiring in the third round.

Schools Rackets.—Rugby (D. S. Milford and G. Goodbody) beat Radley (S. Dawnay and A. Blair) in the final of the public schools rackets championship at Queen's Club on Saturday.

Mitchell Beats Duncan.—After holding a lead of five strokes at the ninth hole, George Duncan was beaten by three strokes by Abe Mitchell at Hanger Hill on Saturday. Mitchell went round in 75.

Cricket at the Oval.—A two days' trial match for Surrey's young players began at the Oval on Saturday. H. Thompson's side knocked up 167, and I. M. Sorensen's team replied with 159 for seven wickets.

Surrey's President.—Lord Midleton is to be proposed as president of the Surrey County Cricket Club in succession to Sir Jeremiah Coleman, Bart., at the club's annual meeting at the Oval on May 17.

King's Prize Winner in Form.—Last year's King's Prize winner, Colonel Marchmont, firing in the London and Middlesex competitions with seven shots at 200, 500 and 600 yards, scored 98 out of a possible 105.

Metropolitan Starters.—Some Great Metropolitan probables are: Arravale (Donoghue), Cylonese (Lister), Sewing Machine (Elliott), Sangrail (Brennan), Adorna (Smirke), Ragout (H. Leach), Donna Inez (Weston). Spes does not run.

Gymnastics Title.—The Individual Gymnastics Championship of England at Manchester Y.M.C.A. Hall on Saturday night was again won by S. Leigh, of Swansea Y.M.C.A., the holder; H. J. Finchett (Birmingham Y.M.C.A.), runner-up last year, was second.

Hendon Lawn Tennis Finals.—At Hendon on Saturday B. I. C. Norton retained the men's singles cup with an easy victory over C. Ramaswami, the All-India lawn tennis international, by 6—2, 6—2, 6—1. Although beaten by Miss Holman by 7—5, 4—6, 6—2, Mrs. McIlquham put up a very fine fight in the women's final.

To-day's Football.—Division II.: Wolverhampton Wanderers v. Hull City (5.45). Division III. (S.): Bristol Rovers v. Norwich City (6.30). Isthmian League: Dulwich Hamlet v. Wycombe Wanderers (6.30); Nunhead v. London Caledonians (6.30). Insurance Offices Cup Final: Motor Union v. Cuaco (at Chelsea) (6.0). Rugby Union: Torquay v. Neath; Pill Harriers v. Cross Keys (6.30).

POST-WAR HEROES

WHEN THE FOOTBALL LEAGUE RESUMED FOLLOWING THE SECOND WORLD WAR, LIVERPOOL EMERGED AS THE MOST FORMIBADLE FORCE. BOASTING THE TALENTS OF ALBERT STUBBINS AND BILLY LIDDELL, THEY CLAIMED THEIR FIFTH LEAGUE CROWN

At the helm: George Kay managed Liverpool to the 1946/47 Division One title

Liverpool's number nine: Albert Stubbins' goals fired Liverpool to the 1946/47 title

FINAL TABLE 1946/47

		Pld	W	D	L	F	A	GA	Pts
1	**Liverpool**	**42**	**25**	**7**	**10**	**84**	**52**	**1.62**	**57**
2	Manchester United	42	22	12	8	95	54	1.76	56
3	Wolves	42	25	6	11	98	56	1.75	56
4	Stoke City	42	24	7	11	90	53	1.70	55
5	Blackpool	42	22	6	14	71	70	1.01	50
6	Sheffield United	42	21	7	14	89	75	1.19	49
7	Preston North End	42	18	11	13	76	74	1.03	47
8	Aston Villa	42	18	9	15	67	53	1.26	45
9	Sunderland	42	18	8	16	65	66	0.98	44
10	Everton	42	17	9	16	62	67	0.93	43
11	Middlesbrough	42	17	8	17	73	68	1.07	42
12	Portsmouth	42	16	9	17	66	60	1.10	41
13	Arsenal	42	16	9	17	72	70	1.03	41
14	Derby County	42	18	5	19	73	79	0.92	41
15	Chelsea	42	16	7	19	69	84	0.82	39
16	Grimsby Town	42	13	12	17	61	82	0.74	38
17	Blackburn Rovers	42	14	8	20	45	53	0.85	36
18	Bolton Wanderers	42	13	8	21	57	69	0.83	34
19	Charlton Athletic	42	11	12	19	57	71	0.80	34
20	Huddersfield Town	42	13	7	22	53	79	0.67	33
21	Brentford	42	9	7	26	45	88	0.51	25
22	Leeds United	42	6	6	30	45	90	0.50	18

Liverpool drank to League win in lemonade

STANLEY CULLIS, grocer's boy who became the greatest centre-half of his day, picked up the black and gold colours he would never wear again (he announced his retirement just before the match) and stared at them for a moment. Then he placed them sadly on the bench.

Instead of the triumph on which he hoped to end his colourful and often splendid career, there was only failure.

And ironically the man who has led Wanderers to so many successes was responsible for Liverpool's second goal, a solo dash by youthful Albert Stubbins, in which he outpaced Cullis all the way.

"I'd no idea Stubbins was so near, and then I saw his red head flash past," Stan said. "He's got amazing speed."

On the championship they missed, Cullis said: "We were on top too long. It was as though Sydney Wooderson had tried to win a race by leading all the way, instead of keeping handy in second or third place.

"It's been the hardest season I've known, and it's ended in the second great disappointment of my career. This was as big a blow as our defeat by Portsmouth in the 1939 Cup Final."

From Ted Vizard, Wolves manager, came the aptest summing-up of the game: "We had our chances, and failed to take them."

Down the corridor in Liverpool's dressing-room players joyfully toasted each other in lemonade, reminded each other that this victory made up for the thrashing Wolves had given them earlier in the season.

Happiest of them all was Cyril Sidlow, who was transferred from Wolverhampton and still lives there.

"They gave us only two chances to score and we grabbed them both," said their captain, Jack Balmer.

JOHN THOMPSON.

Different class: Billy Liddell became a Liverpool legend and played his part in helping the Reds begin the post-war period with some silverware

ADVERTISERS' ANNOUNCEMENTS — THE DAILY MIRROR — ADVERTISERS' ANNOUNCEMENTS Saturday, May 31,

Sports Mirror

ROUND THE CRICKET LEAGUES

Schoolboy hero of his town

SIXTEEN-YEAR-OLD Tommy Dickinson took a day off from playing with his chums in his Grammar School team to turn out for East Lancashire.

Short of players, the club gave a chance to the youngster against Colne, last but one in the League, and Colne thought they were going to pick up some badly needed points when they found a schoolboy was the fast bowler opposing them.

They changed their tune when Tommy went on to bowl. In seven overs he hit the stumps six times at a total cost of nine runs and bundled Colne off to another defeat.

And the next day, the hero of the town, he turned out with his school pals again.

LOWERHOUSE MAKE BEST-EVER BID

FOR nineteen years Arthur Burrows has played for Lowerhouse and never seen them win either the Worsley Cup or the League championship.

"We're not going to be Cinderellas of the League any longer," says Arthur, now skipper of the side. And actions have followed words.

Burnley have been beaten in the Cup competition and the club hold a handy position near the top of the table.

With West Indies fast bowler Martindale in grand form, both with bat and ball, and Arthur himself making good scores, this looks like being their best-ever season.

PEPPER FAVOURITE

WHO'S the first for a thousand runs? is the query from the Central Lancs League.

Hot favourite is Cecil Pepper, Rochdale's Australian star. Cecil, with six completed innings, has scored 363 for an average of 72.

Last year Pepper nearly completed the double. Now, with 33 wickets already, he may achieve the ambition of every League professional.

Luckless Rishton are still fighting to climb from the bottom of the Lancs League.

Their grand Cup win over championship challengers Church has brought fresh confidence to the team.

NOTE THESE COLTS

YORKSHIRE might not be hitting the high spots in County cricket just yet. But wait—they'll be there again.

The colts supply a good reason. Eric Lester, from Scarborough, rattled up 205 against Cheshire, to be followed in the same match by eight wickets for 14 runs by Ron Aspinall, fast bowler from Huddersfield, now playing with Yeadon in the Bradford League.

There are dozens of others coming up in the young Yorkshire, but they've got to go through the League grill properly first—and Yorkshire are prepared to wait.

BEACH TESTS FOR SOCCER KEY GAME

WITH children making sandcastles a few yards away, and hundreds of holidaymakers basking in the sun around them, fifteen sun-tanned young men have sprinted each day this week up and down the grass verging the front at Lytham St. Anne's, near Blackpool. Watching them keenly was a tense figure.

The runners were Wolverhampton players, the watcher, manager Ted Vizard, all of them preparing for today's clash with Liverpool—the match which may settle the First Division championship.

A win and Wolves are undisputed champions; a draw and their hopes rest on the result of Stoke's remaining match.

Defeat—which they don't consider—and the title is gone.

Hospital Leave

MR. BILLY McCONNELL, Liverpool chairman, has special leave of absence from hospital to watch this afternoon's match.

"If Liverpool win, as I think they will, I simply could not be absent," he says.

Travelling with the rest of the players are two who cannot earn championship medals even if their team gain the title.

They are Billy Watkinson and Bob Priday, the reserve wingers, who may play today, but have not enough first-team appearances to earn awards.

"So long as the club wins, it suits us," says Bob.

RADIO GUIDE FOR TODAY'S SOCCER

DIVISION ONE		DIVISION THREE (SOUTH)	
Arsenal	Everton	Mansfield	Orient
Portsmouth	Derby	Northampton	Ipswich
Sheffield U.	Charlton	Port Vale	Southend
Wolves	Liverpool	Walsall	Torquay
DIVISION TWO		**DIVISION THREE (NORTH)**	
Chesterfield	Bury	Accrington	Lincoln
Fulham	Bradford	Bradford C.	Rotherham
Luton	Newport	Chester	Carlisle
Nottingham F.	Plymouth	Hull	Barrow
W.B.A.	Manchester C.	New Brighton	Wrexham
West Ham	Burnley	Rochdale	Tranmere
		Stockport	York

THE BATTLE OF THE BACK GARDEN

A POTATO POINT

Hoe up to a pointed ridge. After that, fill in between the rows with compost, or grass cuttings. Despite planting out of winter kale between the rows, this can be easily and quickly done.

Ray of hope: Welsh international defender Ray Lambert in action in April 1947

THE FRUSTRATING FIFTIES

ALTHOUGH LIVERPOOL REACHED THE FA CUP FINAL IN 1950, THEY WERE RELEGATED TO THE SECOND DIVISION IN 1953/54 AND STRUGGLED TO RECAPTURE FORMER GLORIES DURING A DECADE OF DECLINE

Red men: Liverpool line up for a squad photo in October 1948

Bob and Bill: Paisley and Jones in action at Huddersfield in 1950

Fans' favourites: Cyril Sidlow and Ray Lambert sign autographs

Training day: Eddie Spicer gets in some practice at Anfield as does Phil Taylor (left)

King Billy: Liddell in training

Bob's the job: Bob Paisley in April 1950

Saver Sidlow: Welsh international goalkeeper Cyril Sidlow in action during the 1949/50 season

"There were only two competitions to go for then – the FA Cup and the league. There was plenty of pressure of course trying to win these competitons, but nothing like the lads are subjected to today"
– Bob Paisley speaking in the 1980s

Finalists: The 1949/50 team that reached the FA Cup final

Heading for a fall: Tommy Younger cannot prevent Dick White's deflection help Worcester City inflict a famous FA Cup giantkilling on the Reds in January 1959

Head boys: Coach Bob Paisley leads Billy Liddell and team-mates in a training drill at Melwood in August 1956

Climbing high: Billy Liddell contests possession with Sheffield United goalkeeper Alan Hodgkinson in April 1958

Close control: Geoff Twentyman, who would go on to become a key part of the club's scouting network, in January 1951

SHANKLY'S SIXTIES

AFTER TAKING THE ANFIELD REINS LATE IN 1959, BILL SHANKLY SET ABOUT THE BUSINESS OF TRANSFORMING LIVERPOOL INTO THE BEST TEAM IN THE LAND DURING THE SIXTIES. THESE WERE THE DAYS THAT HELPED SHAPE A FOOTBALL DYNASTY

Ready for action: Liverpool line up for a team photo at Melwood ahead of the 1962/63 season. They are, back row, from left: Gordon Milne, Gerry Byrne, Tommy Leishman, Jim Furnell, Tommy Lawrence, Ron Yeats, Ronnie Moran. Centre: Kevin Lewis, Roger Hunt, Ian St John, Jimmy Melia, Alan A'Court. Front row: Alan Jones, Alf Arrowsmith, Johnny Morrissey and Ian Callaghan

At the Orient: Goalkeeper Jim Furnell keeps out a shot during the 2-2 draw at Leyton Orient in March 1962. Liverpool went on to win promotion back to the top-flight as Division Two champions that season

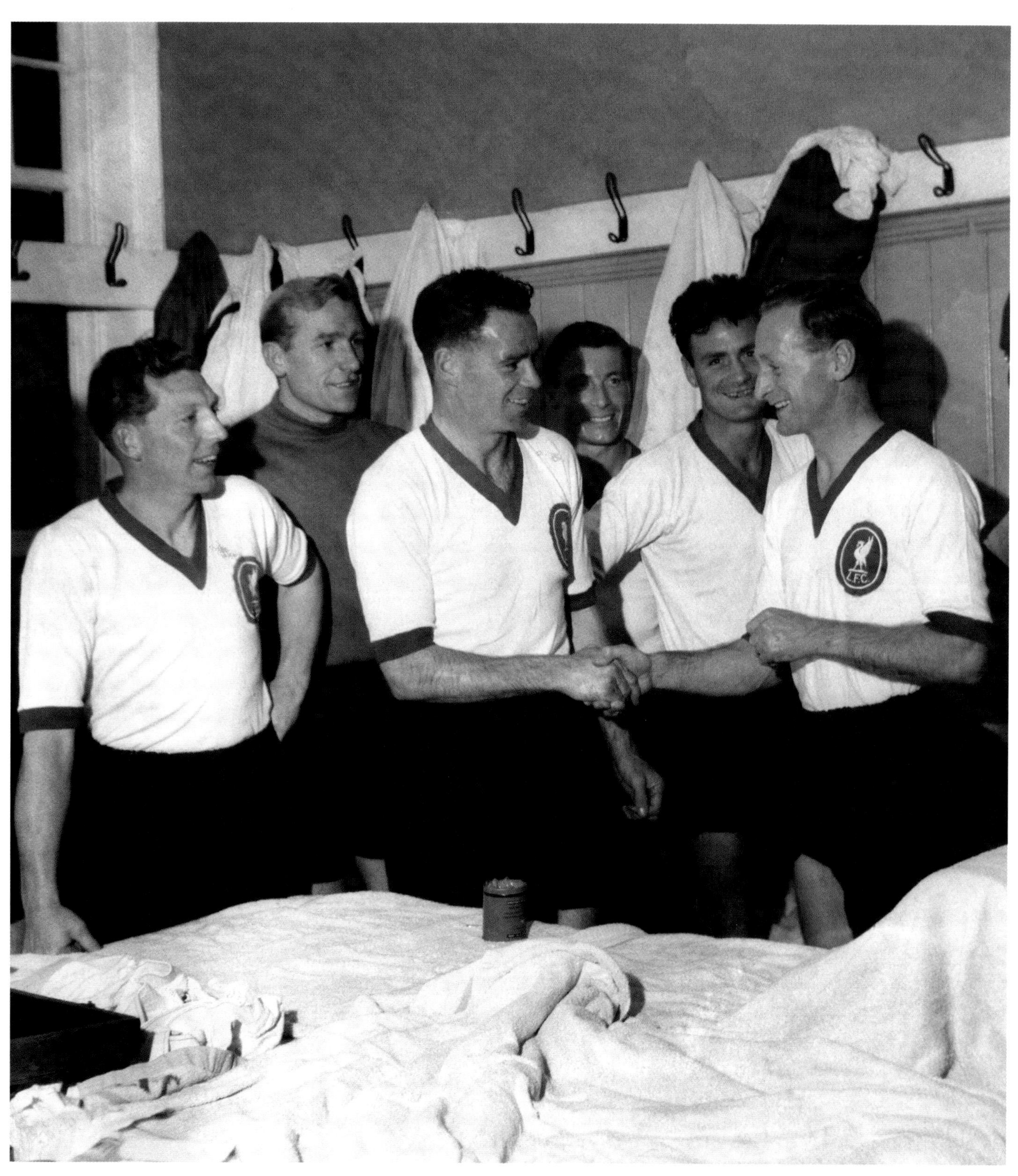

Liddellpool: Stars of English football such as Jimmy Armfield, Bert Trautmann, Jimmy McIlroy and Tom Finney wore a Liverbird upon their chests for Billy Liddell's testimonial match at Anfield in September 1960

Champions: Taking the applause of the crowd from the directors' box after winning their first Division One title in 17 years. Pictured left to right are: Ian St John, Gordon Milne, Peter Thompson, Ian Callaghan, Alf Arrowsmith, Bill Shankly, Ron Yeats, Tommy Lawrence, Gerry Byrne, Roger Hunt and Willie Stevenson

"In the late '50s we were a happy-go-lucky, slap-happy crowd. The height of the directors' ambitions was to get into the First Division and they'd have been quite happy just to get there and go along three or four places off the bottom but Bill was determined to change that"

– Bob Paisley

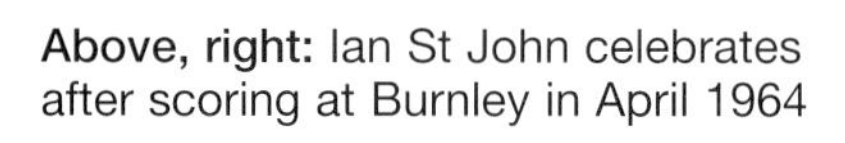

Above, right: Ian St John celebrates after scoring at Burnley in April 1964

Fab four: Ian St John, Ron Yeats and Billy Liddell join Ken Dodd to pose as The Beatles in December 1963

Sweet success: Celebrating in the Anfield dressing rooms after beating Arsenal 5-0 to clinch the 1963/64 league title

FINAL TABLE 1963/64

		Pld	W	D	L	F	A	GA	Pts
1	**Liverpool**	**42**	**26**	**5**	**11**	**92**	**45**	**2.04**	**57**
2	Manchester United	42	23	7	12	90	62	1.45	53
3	Everton	42	21	10	11	84	64	1.31	52
4	Tottenham Hotspur	42	22	7	13	97	81	1.20	51
5	Chelsea	42	20	10	12	72	56	1.29	50
6	Sheffield Wednesday	42	19	11	12	84	67	1.25	49
7	Blackburn Rovers	42	18	10	14	89	65	1.37	46
8	Arsenal	42	17	11	14	90	82	1.10	45
9	Burnley	42	17	10	15	71	64	1.11	44
10	West Brom	42	16	11	15	70	61	1.15	43
11	Leicester City	42	16	11	15	61	58	1.05	43
12	Sheffield United	42	16	11	15	61	64	0.95	43
13	Nottingham Forest	42	16	9	17	64	68	0.94	41
14	West Ham United	42	14	12	16	69	74	0.93	40
15	Fulham	42	13	13	16	58	65	0.89	39
16	Wolves	42	12	15	15	70	80	0.88	39
17	Stoke City	42	14	10	18	77	78	0.99	38
18	Blackpool	42	13	9	20	52	73	0.71	35
19	Aston Villa	42	11	12	19	62	71	0.87	34
20	Birmingham City	42	11	7	24	54	92	0.59	29
21	Bolton Wanderers	42	10	8	24	48	80	0.60	28
22	Ipswich Town	42	9	7	26	56	121	0.46	25

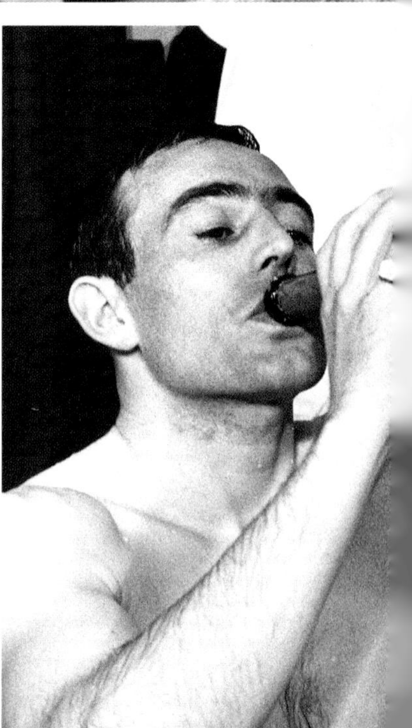

Guard of honour: Chelsea applaud league champions Liverpool as the team runs out ahead of the Reds' final home league game of the 1965/66 season. Tommy Lawrence is followed by Gerry Byrne, Ian Callaghan and Tommy Smith. The players celebrated with a pint in the local (below)

Bottom: Bill Shankly pops into the treatment room in March 1966, left, while right, Ian St John and Roger Hunt toast their title success

Liverpool football team looks in at the local

This is one of Britain's top teams of the moment taking time out at the local. The day after this picture was taken they were licking Everton five goals to one in the all important Merseyside derby. Last Tuesday they defeated Celtic 2-0 in the semi-final of the European Cup-Winners' Cup.

They don't spend a lot of time in pubs, and when they go there they don't drink heavily. But the odd pint or shandy in the local means a lot to them. "If we didn't have a break now and then, we'd go stale" their captain says. "And a pub is a great place to unwind after you've been keyed up for a big match."

In the picture from left to right: Peter Thompson, Tom Smith, Ian Callaghan, Gerry Byrne, Gordon Milne, Ron Yeats, Geoff Strong, Roger Hunt, Ian St John and Tommy Lawrence. If you wonder where Bill Stevenson was when the picture was taken, remember that somebody has to be at the bar getting in the drinks.

Like the Liverpool lads—look in at the local

FINAL TABLE 1965/66

		Pld	W	D	L	F	A	GA	Pts
1	**Liverpool**	**42**	**26**	**9**	**7**	**79**	**34**	**2.32**	**61**
2	Leeds United	42	23	9	10	79	38	2.08	55
3	Burnley	42	24	7	11	79	47	1.68	55
4	Manchester United	42	18	15	9	84	59	1.42	51
5	Chelsea	42	22	7	13	65	53	1.23	51
6	West Bromwich Albion	42	19	12	11	91	69	1.32	50
7	Leicester City	42	21	7	14	80	65	1.23	49
8	Tottenham Hotspur	42	16	12	14	75	66	1.14	44
9	Sheffield United	42	16	11	15	56	59	0.95	43
10	Stoke City	42	15	12	15	65	64	1.02	42
11	Everton	42	15	11	16	56	62	0.90	41
12	West Ham United	42	15	9	18	70	83	0.84	39
13	Blackpool	42	14	9	19	55	65	0.85	37
14	Arsenal	42	12	13	17	62	75	0.83	37
15	Newcastle United	42	14	9	19	50	63	0.79	37
16	Aston Villa	42	15	6	21	69	80	0.86	36
17	Sheffield Wednesday	42	14	8	20	56	66	0.85	36
18	Nottingham Forest	42	14	8	20	56	72	0.78	36
19	Sunderland	42	14	8	20	51	72	0.71	36
20	Fulham	42	14	7	21	67	85	0.79	35
21	Northampton Town	42	10	13	19	55	92	0.60	33
22	Blackburn Rovers	42	8	4	30	57	88	0.65	20

The Saint: Ian St John in action at Fulham in February 1967, below, and bottom, enjoying a training session with Roger Hunt, Jimmy Melia and Alan A'Court

Stepping out: Ron Yeats leads the Reds out for their Division One match against Manchester United at Anfield in March 1967

Team talk: Bill Shankly chats with Preston and England legend Tom Finney

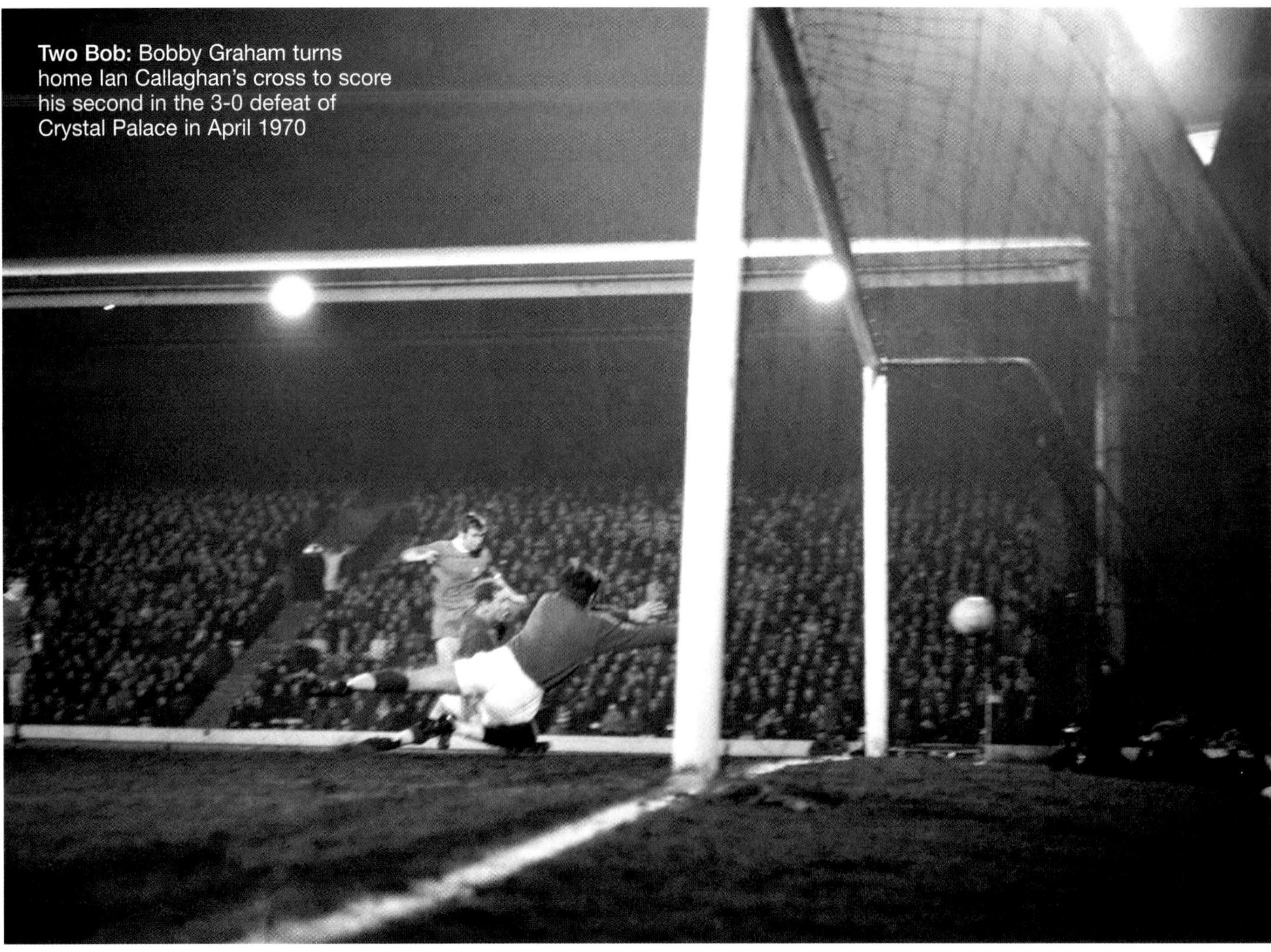

Two Bob: Bobby Graham turns home Ian Callaghan's cross to score his second in the 3-0 defeat of Crystal Palace in April 1970

THE SOARING SEVENTIES

SHANKLY'S RED REVOLUTION WAS IN FULL SWING AS A NEW DECADE OF SUCCESS DAWNED AT ANFIELD. ALONG WITH HIS SUCCESSOR BOB PAISLEY, THE MANAGERIAL MASTERMINDS BUILT A FOOTBALLING ESTABLISHMENT WHICH WOULD PROPEL THE CLUB TO GREATER GLORY

Bobby dazzler: Graham celebrates scoring his first against Palace

Ref justice: Emlyn Hughes, Kevin Keegan and Manchester United keeper Alex Stepney argue a disallowed goal in 1971

Derby joy: Celebrations following victory over Everton

Gesture: Bill Shankly salutes the Kop as Leicester visit Anfield during the final stages of the successful 72/73 season

Prize guys: Emlyn Hughes and Phil Thompson show off the league trophy

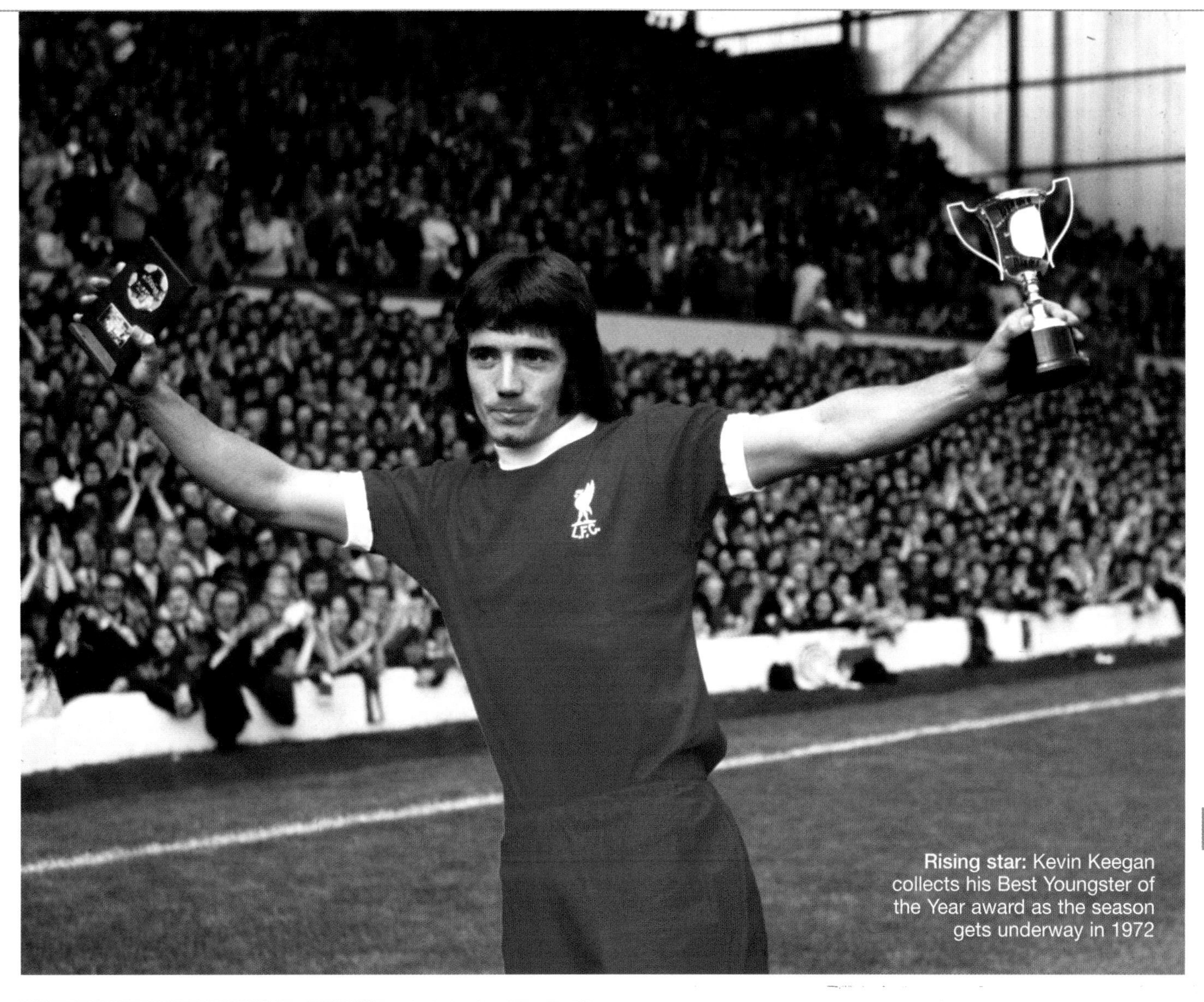

Rising star: Kevin Keegan collects his Best Youngster of the Year award as the season gets underway in 1972

Fan-tastic: Supporters celebrate Liverpool's First Division success and (right) the Daily Mirror proclaims Shankly's men the champions

Tuesday, April 24, 1973
Telephone: (STD code 01)—353 0246

Ee, aye addio.. Shanks' men do it again

CHAMPS!

By KEVIN MOSELEY

BILL SHANKLY'S Liverpool are League champions in all but name. Barring a sensational upset no one can take the title from them after yesterday's 2—0 victory over Leeds at happy Anfield.

Arsenal—four points behind with two games to play—have only the faintest chance of overhauling them on goal average. And Liverpool would have to lose their last match at home to Leicester on Saturday.

They deserve it, says Revie

Don Revie, whose Leeds side needed a win to keep their hopes alive, said last night: "It's Liverpool's title. They deserve it for their consistency."

Liverpool skipper Tommy Smith said: "As far as I'm concerned it's all over. I don't think we'll be caught." And even Arsenal boss Bertie Mee conceded after a 2—2 draw at Southampton: "We need a miracle now."

Jubilant

A capacity crowd of over 55,000 at Anfield hailed goals from Peter Cormack and Kevin Keegan. A jubilant Shankly said: "I'm delighted. The boys played a magnificent game. It was a great match.

"One thing that pleased me this weekend was the way Everton took their game against Arsenal so seriously and helped us by earning a draw."

BRENTFORD promoted last season, have been relegated back to the Fourth Division after a 4—1 thrashing at Wrexham.

SOUTHPORT clinched the Fourth Division championship with a draw against Hartlepool.

REFEREE Keith Styles was knocked to the ground and kicked by angry fans at Port Vale after Bolton had ended Vale's chances of promotion to the Second Division by drawing 2—2.

Styles hobbled off and was treated by medical staff. He refused to comment later.

TOP POSITIONS

	P	W	D	L	F	A	Pts.
Liverpool	41	25	9	7	72	42	59
Arsenal ...	40	22	11	7	54	36	55
Leeds ...	39	20	11	8	63	39	51

CHAMPS! . . . first scorer Peter Cormack

CHAMPS! . . . second scorer Kevin Keegan.

Pictures: MONTE FRESCO

FRANK McGHEE AT ANFIELD: NIGEL CLARKE AT THE DELL—PAGES 30, 31

MAL: WE CAN ESCAPE

BOTTOM POSITIONS

	P	W	D	L	F	A	Pts.
Norwich .	40	10	10	20	34	60	30
C. Palace	40	8	12	20	37	54	28
WBA ...	40	9	10	21	35	57	28

MALCOLM ALLISON, Crystal Palace's new and controversial manager, gave his side a vote of confidence last night on the eve of tonight's critical match at Norwich. "I believe the Palace players have the ability to keep the club in the First Division by winning at Norwich," he said.

"I won't accept relegation is inevitable until the final results are in."

Allison—and Palace—were given fresh hope with the news of Norwich's defeat at Wolves yesterday.

No let-up for Norwich

By HARRY MILLER: Wolves 3, Norwich 0

NORWICH made the cross-country trek home to Norfolk last night knowing that another season of First Division football is a promised land still to be sighted and secured.

They were sunk yesterday — and in the rain-lashed conditions that is the most appropriate description—by two goals from young Wolves reserve Alan Sunderland and another by John Richards.

The game started and finished in torrential rain and was played out on a strength-sapping, muddy mess of a pitch.

Luck and the heroics of goalkeeper Kevin Keelan prevented Norwich from falling behind until the 53rd minute. Then Sunderland played a one-two with the superb Richards before coolly slotting home a low shot.

Wolves, driven forward by the powerful Mike Bailey, scored again after 76 minutes.

Richards, the young man with a definite England future, scored his 34th first team goal of the season with a snap shot after John McAlle's drive had been deflected to him off Duncan Forbes.

Norwich, visibly sagging, conceded a third goal eight minutes from the end. Richards, almost arrogantly, headed down a long David Wagstaffe ball for Sunderland to slot it in.

David Cross and Graham Paddon, Norwich's two leading scorers, were both missing from this match because of injury.

Manager Ron Saunders said: "I don't know whether either will be fit to face Palace."

Club captain Paddy Mulligan responded to Allison's comments by saying: "No one can blame the manager for our poor results in the last few weeks.

"He has seen Palace at their very worst. The pressure has been telling on a few of us.

Spirit

"A couple of months ago we were playing really well—with flair and imagination. But the spirit within the side is still good and that's the important thing.

"We can—and must—win at Norwich. And we have the comfort of knowing we have the best goal average of the three teams down at the bottom."

ANOTHER JAIL TERM FOR TIMOTHY LEARY

Dr. Timothy Leary, "high priest" of LSD, sentenced in California early today to from six months to five years in prison for escaping from California Men's Colony three years ago. Sentence to run consecutively with original ten-year term for possessing "pot."

THE WINNING Racing Mirror FOUR PAGES 26, 27, 28, 29

Printed and Published by THE DAILY MIRROR NEWSPAPERS Ltd. (01-353 0246) at, and for I P C Newspapers Ltd., Holborn Circus, London, EC1P 1DQ. Registered at the Post Office as a newspaper

K7

"Above all, I would like to be remembered as a man who was selfless, who strove and worried so that others could share the glory, and who built up a family of people who could hold their heads up high and say, 'We're Liverpool'"

– Bill Shankly

PAGE 30 DAILY MIRROR, Tuesday, April 24, 1973

SALUTE THE NEW CHAMPS

SHANKLY ENDS SEVEN-YEAR ITCH

FRANK McGHEE reports a Liverpool triumph

BILL SHANKLY ... celebrates with a cup of tea.

Kevin nips in to end Leeds title challenge

Liverpool 2, Leeds Utd 0

LIVERPOOL are now close enough to the gleaming prize of the League championship to breathe on it, polish it and clear a place for it in their trophy cabinet. It is theirs. They have earned it. They deserve it.

And only statisticians or mathematicians, only those with computers where they should have hearts will attempt to dispute it.

All right, if Liverpool don't get another point from their remaining game at home against lowly Leicester, and Arsenal win high-scoring away matches against West Ham and Leeds, the title might still go to Highbury.

But then if my Aunt Mabel had a slightly different physique, she'd be my uncle.

Dispute

Certainly no one at ecstatic Anfield yesterday was prepared to discuss all the maze of ifs and buts and maybes.

No one was prepared to dispute that Bill Shankly's side are champions again after a seven-year gap — and among those who were not arguing were the Leeds United team.

They lined up sportingly on either side of the players' tunnel at the end to salute and applaud the men who had won the prize they themselves most cherish.

Their manager, Don Revie, said afterwards: "I know I speak for all the lads when I say that if we couldn't do it there's no one we'd sooner see as champions than Liverpool."

Leeds had, in fact, crammed all their own chances of staying in the race into three hectic minutes of the first half when Liverpool 'keeper Ray Clemence had to make fine saves from Peter Lorimer and Joe Jordan.

From that moment, Liverpool were in charge of the last hour of a game of breakneck pace, breathtaking excitement and ear-shattering enthusiasm from a crammed Kop crowd.

It was typical of the numbers of men they threw forward to exert inexorable pressure on Leeds that two defenders—Phil Thompson and Chris Lawler—were involved in the build-up for the vital breakthrough goal in the 47th minute.

Little Kevin Keegan finally flicked it through to his inside forward colleague, Peter Cormack who scored.

In midfield the skill of Billy Bremner and the massive composure of Paul Madeley did stiffen Leeds' resolve briefly after a whole series of Liverpool attacks had threatened to swamp them halfway through the second half.

But, frankly, Leeds had too many key men missing—notably Johnny Giles and Mick Jones—to counter-attack effectively.

An Allan Clarke shot hooked just too high is the only second-half chance I can remember, while Liverpool had at least half a dozen—with the inspirational figure of the galloping Emlyn Hughes once again their driving force.

Yet the second goal they scored had a slightly freakish element about it.

Leeds 'keeper David Harvey became inextricably entangled with a defender after parrying a cross from Cormack. Keegan, resisting a lusty attempt to flatten him snapped up the loose ball to make it 2—0.

That ended a game which Bill Shankly, with typical enthusiasm, described as "one of the best seen in Britain this season, if not for years."

Facing the facts . . . We've made it, beams Liverpool's Emlyn Hughes. We've had it, admits Leeds' Billy Bremner. Pictures: MONTE FRESCO

DAILY MIRROR, Tuesday, April 24, 1973 PAGE 31

Ball mourns as Arsenal bow out of League race

NIGEL CLARKE sees Mee's men lose the race

Southampton 2, Arsenal 2

ALAN BALL'S slow, sad walk back to the sanctuary of the dressing room at the end yesterday mirrored Arsenal's despair as Southampton finally put the League championship beyond their reach.

The little midfield man, head bowed in sorrow, was close to tears as physiotherapist Fred Street escorted him off the pitch, a comforting arm around his shoulders. For once again Arsenal look certain to finish with nothing to show from a season of dedicated trophy hunting.

Manager Bertie Mee, studying the top of the table that sees his club four points behind leaders Liverpool and with an inferior goal average of 1·5 to 1·7, said: "I wish my name was Shankly."

Asked if Arsenal are now conceding the title, he answered: "A very good question, but we now need a miracle."

It was Bobby Stokes, a young reserve drafted in to deputise for England's Mike Channon, who scored the goals that destroyed Arsenal's dream by twice hauling them back from the lead.

And Stokes's second came with the kind of good fortune that so often has been the sole right of Arsenal this season.

Sliding

As he cut down the left in the fifty-eighth minute and shot, Peter Simpson's sliding tackle diverted the ball just inside the near post with goalkeeper Bob Wilson going the other way.

That levelled the game and it was Stokes who, five minutes from time, so nearly got his hat-trick and a goal which would have buried Arsenal with a shot from close in that skimmed the bar.

Arsenal had gone ahead as early as the second minute when Ball set up a chance that Charlie George took from close in, his shot being fumbled by 'keeper Eric Martin as he went to his left.

Within four minutes Southampton were level when Stokes, unmarked, scored from a yard.

After that it was George's aggression in midfield that sent Arsenal pushing forward and in the twentieth minute they went ahead again.

George was lying flat in the penalty area, felled by a mighty clearance from Southampton's Steve Mills when Eddie Kelly crossed from the left. John Radford rose unchallenged to drive a header low past Martin.

Enjoyed

Ball had two chances to put Arsenal further ahead but missed them and Arsenal were never again allowed the freedom they enjoyed in the first half as Terry Paine and Brian O'Neil seized command for Saints.

When the final whistle went little Ball stood motionless for a minute, holding his head in his hands as he and his team mates realised at last their pursuit of Liverpool was now all over.

Charlie George slams Arsenal's first goal at the Dell, but it's all academic as Bertie Mee's men fail in their title bid.

WORLD WIDE

... debut for Exeter in the Easter Trophy victory over Poole. Mauger scored nine points in a 49—29 second leg win. Exeter triumphed 86—70 on aggregate.

SNOOKER star Alex "Hurricane" Higgins lost his world title when he was whipped 27-17 by Australian Eddie Charlton in yesterday's semi-final of the Park Drive championships in Manchester. Charlton meets Ray Reardon (Stoke) who stormed back to beat John Spencer (Radcliffe) 23-22.

WEST INDIES were struggling at 193 for five, despite a defiant 73 from opener Roy Fredericks, 226 behind Australia's 419 for eight declared at the end of the rain-curtailed third day in the fifth and final Test at Port of Spain. The Aussies hold a 2—0 lead in the series.

TODAY'S CRICKET

DAILY MIRROR LEISURE GUIDE

TEENY-BOPPERS THRILL SEXTON

By JACK STEGGLES

Cripps in uproar at the Den

Millwall 1 A Villa 1

MILLWALL favourite Harry Cripps was involved in a 75th-minute flare-up with Villa striker Ray Graydon that ended in Graydon being sent off.

IT'S FERGUSON THE HERO

Birmingham 0, West Ham 0

BOBBY FERGUSON, fearless as ever, salvaged West Ham a point at Birmingham with two flying second-half saves.

Ferguson, back after missing two games with a neck injury, flew to his left to clutch a Garry Pendrey drive ...

Luton get stuck in their mud

Bert blunders—and Brighton look doomed

GREYHOUND RESULTS AND SPORTS SUMMARY

PETCHEY: IT'S BEEN A TOUGH SEASON

By KEVIN MOSELEY

Orient 3, Fulham 2

ORIENT'S relegation fears disappeared with their seventh successive home victory in this thriller.

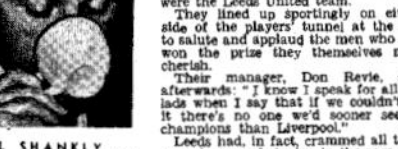

TONIGHT'S FIXTURES

Aldershot get set for the champers

WATFORD SAFE

RESULTS, SCORERS AND TABLES

FIRST DIVISION | SECOND DIVISION | THIRD DIVISION | FOURTH DIVISION

RUGBY UNION | RUGBY LEAGUE | SWIMMING | RALLYING

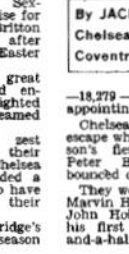

FINAL TABLE 1972/73

		Pld	W	D	L	F	A	GA	Pts
1	**Liverpool**	**42**	**25**	**10**	**7**	**72**	**42**	**1.71**	**60**
2	Arsenal	42	23	11	8	57	43	1.33	57
3	Leeds United	42	21	11	10	71	45	1.58	53
4	Ipswich Town	42	17	14	11	55	45	1.22	48
5	Wolves	42	18	11	13	66	54	1.22	47
6	West Ham United	42	17	12	13	67	53	1.26	46
7	Derby County	42	19	8	15	56	54	1.04	46
8	Tottenham Hotspur	42	16	13	13	58	48	1.21	45
9	Newcastle United	42	16	13	13	60	51	1.18	45
10	Birmingham City	42	15	12	15	53	54	0.98	42
11	Manchester City	42	15	11	16	57	60	0.95	41
12	Chelsea	42	13	14	15	49	51	0.96	40
13	Southampton	42	11	18	13	47	52	0.90	40
14	Sheffield United	42	15	10	17	51	59	0.86	40
15	Stoke City	42	14	10	18	61	56	1.09	38
16	Leicester City	42	10	17	15	40	46	0.87	37
17	Everton	42	13	11	18	41	49	0.84	37
18	Manchester United	42	12	13	17	44	60	0.73	37
19	Coventry City	42	13	9	20	40	55	0.73	35
20	Norwich City	42	11	10	21	36	63	0.57	32
21	Crystal Palace	42	9	12	21	41	58	0.71	30
22	West Bromwich Albion	42	9	10	23	38	62	0.61	28

Left, above: Chris Lawler, Ian Callaghan and Tommy Smith celebrate with the league trophy in the Anfield changing rooms following victory over Leicester, while (left, below) Smith joins Emlyn Hughes in parading their prize to the fans

Opposite: Shankly collects his Manager of the Year award after guiding the Reds to their eighth league title

Managerial masterminds: Shankly studies the action alongside Brian Clough

Funny old game: Comedian Jimmy Tarbuck shows his allegiance

Safe hands: Ray Clemence springs into action as he keeps West Ham out during a goalless draw at Upton Park in February 1975

Closing in: Kevin Keegan forces Chelsea keeper Peter Bonetti into a save in September 1973

Signing in: Ray Kennedy putting pen to paper as he agrees a £180,000 move from Arsenal overlooked by the Liverpool board and Bill Shankly, who announced his retirement later that day

Captain's toast: Emlyn Hughes leads the celebrations at Wolves where Liverpool were confirmed as league champions in May 1976

Loyal servant: Ian Callaghan

FINAL TABLE 1975/76

		Pld	W	D	L	F	A	GA	Pts
1	**Liverpool**	**42**	**23**	**14**	**5**	**66**	**31**	**2.13**	**60**
2	Queens Park Rangers	42	24	11	7	67	33	2.03	59
3	Manchester United	42	23	10	9	68	42	1.62	56
4	Derby County	42	21	11	10	75	58	1.29	53
5	Leeds United	42	21	9	12	65	46	1.41	51
6	Ipswich Town	42	16	14	12	54	48	1.13	46
7	Leicester City	42	13	19	10	48	51	0.94	45
8	Manchester City	42	16	11	15	64	46	1.39	43
9	Tottenham Hotspur	42	14	15	13	63	63	1.00	43
10	Norwich City	42	16	10	16	58	58	1.00	42
11	Everton	42	15	12	15	60	66	0.91	42
12	Stoke City	42	15	11	16	48	50	0.96	41
13	Middlesbrough	42	15	10	17	46	45	1.02	40
14	Coventry City	42	13	14	15	47	57	0.83	40
15	Newcastle United	42	15	9	18	71	62	1.15	39
16	Aston Villa	42	11	17	14	51	59	0.86	39
17	Arsenal	42	13	10	19	47	53	0.89	36
18	West Ham United	42	13	10	19	48	71	0.68	36
19	Birmingham City	42	13	7	22	57	75	0.76	33
20	Wolves	42	10	10	22	51	68	0.75	30
21	Burnley	42	9	10	23	43	66	0.65	28
22	Sheffield United	42	6	10	26	33	82	0.40	22

"In my time at the club there were perhaps three players who, through their consistency, epitomised the Liverpool Way more than anyone. Ian Callaghan, Kevin Keegan, and of course, Emlyn Hughes"

– John Toshack

PAGE 30 DAILY MIRROR, Thursday, May 6, 1976

ALWAYS AT THE HEART OF THE MATTER

FRANK McGHEE THE VOICE OF SPORT

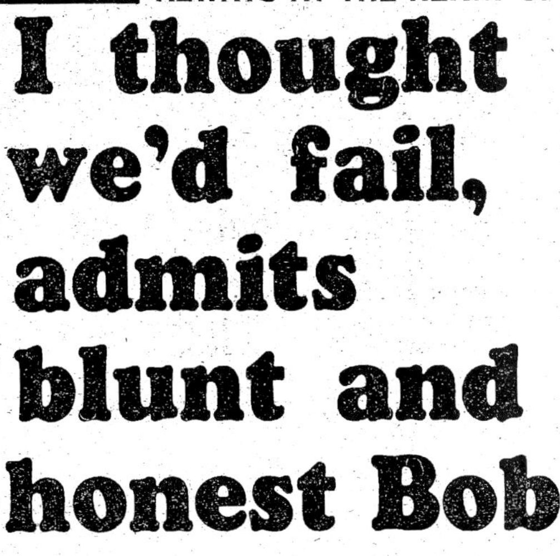

I thought we'd fail, admits blunt and honest Bob

BOB PAISLEY, the blunt, honest, home-spun man who manages new League champions, Liverpool, doesn't believe his team has sufficient skill.

He didn't really believe they would win the title this year—he felt certain Queen's Park Rangers would.

Paisley dropped those considerably controversial remarks into a quiet conversation he had with me very late on Tuesday night. It was rather like dropping a hand-grenade into a pond—and with much the same effect.

But when this stocky Geordie with the lived-in, stepped-on face went more deeply into what he meant, something very important about the character of the man and his champions emerged.

An hour after his team clinched the title at Wolverhampton, he told me: "I say we haven't got enough skill because you can't have enough. We've got plenty but however much you have, you can do with more.

Dedication

"What my players do have more of than any other team in the First Division is determination and dedication. The sooner the England team realise and accept how important these are, the better it will be for our international football future.

"I am tired of hearing and reading about players with other sides who are supposed to have such marvellous skills and show them one week out of six. They wouldn't last beyond the first couple of off-form games with us."

What about his apparent lack of faith in his team's ability to take the trophy they won — and deserved—so clearly?

Strategy

"I looked at the situation a month or so ago, the points we had, the programme we faced, the situation Q P R were in, and decided it probably wasn't on.

"I didn't of course let anyone else know what I felt, but that was the main reason I re-arranged this closing match against Wolves for after the season had finished.

"I thought it would be a good way of keeping the team in shape for the U E F A Cup Final second leg against Bruges. I thought we would lose the title and win the cup."

Bob Paisley smiled with pure pleasure when he recalled what made him change his mind.

"I have always made it a policy never to criticise other teams or other managers, and I know now I'm right.

"I've got to be grateful to John Bond, the Norwich manager, for saying that it would be a bad thing for English football if Liverpool won the title and a great thing if Q P R did it instead.

Resentment

"I didn't have to motivate our players after that. John Bond did it for me."

He is right. Bond's comments lit a fire of resentment under Liverpool's players that was still smouldering even after they had won the title at Wolverhampton. It still might take them some time to appreciate what a favour the Norwich manager did them!

Kevin Keegan (left) meets Gerry Francis. *Picture: MIKE MALONEY.*

ENGLAND FIRST—KEVIN

By GRAHAM BAKER

KEVIN KEEGAN, who walked out on England a year ago, missed Liverpool's League championship celebrations as a sign of his dedication to international duty.

While the rest of the Liverpool party made merry after clinching their ninth League title with a 3—1 win at Wolves on Tuesday night, Keegan was heading home to the village of Hendre in North Wales.

He arrived at 2.0 a.m. and had four hours sleep before leaving for London to join the rest of the England party for the Home International championship.

Keegan said: "I was disappointed to miss the celebrations, but playing for England must come first.

"Anybody who says it means nothing to play for England needs their backside kicked."

Keegan, the Footballer of the Year, scored the 75th-minute equaliser at Molineux that ensured Queen's Park Rangers finished as runners-up in the First Division.

Yet there were broad smiles on the faces of both players when Keegan met Rangers skipper Gerry Francis with the rest of the England party yesterday.

Tunnel vision: Kevin Keegan focused as he runs out at Anfield

Above: The Daily Mirror reports Bob Paisley's surprise at winning the title in 1976 and (below) previewing the championship-clincher for the Reds as they travelled to Wolves on May 4

WW DAILY MIRROR, Tuesday, May 4, 1976 PAGE 27

ALWAYS AT THE HEART OF THE MATTER

FRANK McGHEE THE VOICE OF SPORT

I'd hate to swap places with McGarry tonight

LIVERPOOL are the one team in the First Division this season I would hate to have to play if I were the manager of a club needing a victory to stand any chance of avoiding relegation.

Bill McGarry of Wolves is in that fraught and frightening situation tonight.

BOB PAISLEY

THE TITLE CRUNCH

RELEGATION CRUNCH

PROMOTION SCENE

BOBBY OUT TO ROAST THEM!

By TOM LYONS

CARDIFF, one point away from promotion, can expect no favours when they face Bury at Gigg Lane tonight.

Adamant

TONIGHT'S SOCCER

INTERNATIONAL SCENE

Cap that! Welsh team manager Mike Smith (left) with some of his players at their hotel in Llanwern. *Picture: RON HARDING.*

Hammer in the Welsh works

Trenter in for Wales

CLIVE STRIKES AND NEWPORT GO CRASHING

Brad City 3, Newport 0

REVENGE BID BY MEADE

adidas

umbro
umbro

Above: Ian Callaghan celebrates his 800th appearance for Liverpool in February 1977. He turned out a further 57 times for the club, setting a record which still stands

Left, below: Ray Kennedy and Emlyn Hughes celebrate taking Liverpool into double figures at Anfield with their tenth title victory, while (left, top) the rest of the squad line up with manager Bob Paisley and the other trophies they won that season – the European Cup and the Charity Shield

FINAL TABLE 1976/77

		Pld	W	D	L	F	A	GD	Pts
1	**Liverpool**	**42**	**23**	**11**	**8**	**62**	**33**	**29**	**57**
2	Manchester City	42	21	14	7	60	34	26	56
3	Ipswich Town	42	22	8	12	66	39	27	52
4	Aston Villa	42	22	7	13	76	50	26	51
5	Newcastle United	42	18	13	11	64	49	15	49
6	Manchester United	42	18	11	13	71	62	9	47
7	West Bromwich Albion	42	16	13	13	62	56	6	45
8	Arsenal	42	16	11	15	64	59	5	43
9	Everton	42	14	14	14	62	64	-2	42
10	Leeds United	42	15	12	15	48	51	-3	42
11	Leicester City	42	12	18	12	47	60	-13	42
12	Middlesbrough	42	14	13	15	40	45	-5	41
13	Birmingham City	42	13	12	17	63	61	2	38
14	Queens Park Rangers	42	13	12	17	47	52	-5	38
15	Derby County	42	9	19	14	50	55	-5	37
16	Norwich City	42	14	9	19	47	64	-17	37
17	West Ham United	42	11	14	17	46	65	-19	36
18	Bristol City	42	11	13	18	38	48	-10	35
19	Coventry City	42	10	15	17	48	59	-11	35
20	Sunderland	42	11	12	19	46	54	-8	34
21	Stoke City	42	10	14	18	28	51	-23	34
22	Tottenham Hotspur	42	12	9	21	48	72	-24	33

Caped crusaders: Kevin Keegan and John Toshack dressed as Batman and Robin

Head man: Kenny Dalglish making his Liverpool debut in the 1977 Charity Shield

Relaxing: Graeme Souness winds down after the '78 season

Dressed to kill: Ray Kennedy as gangster Al Capone

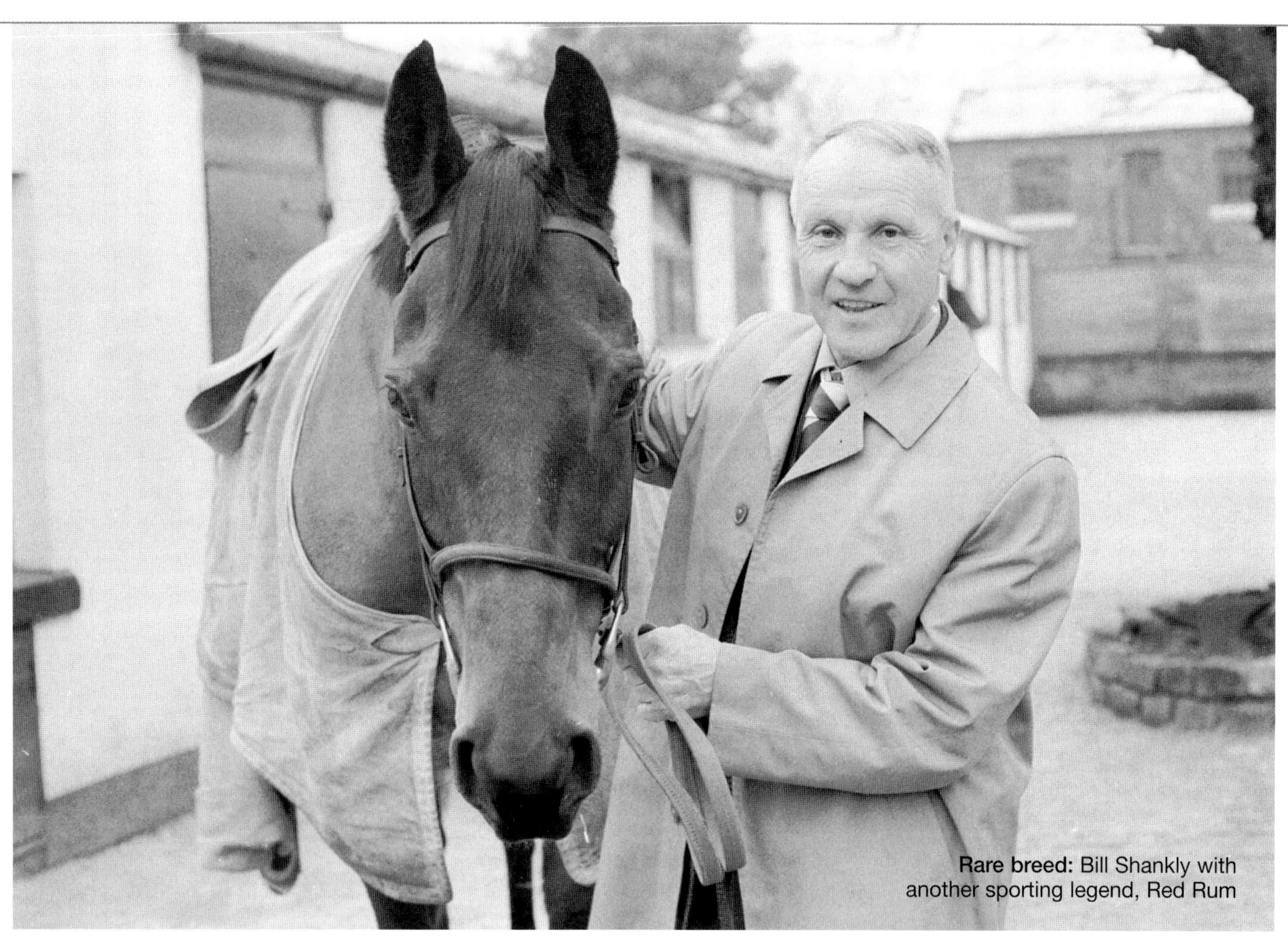

Rare breed: Bill Shankly with another sporting legend, Red Rum

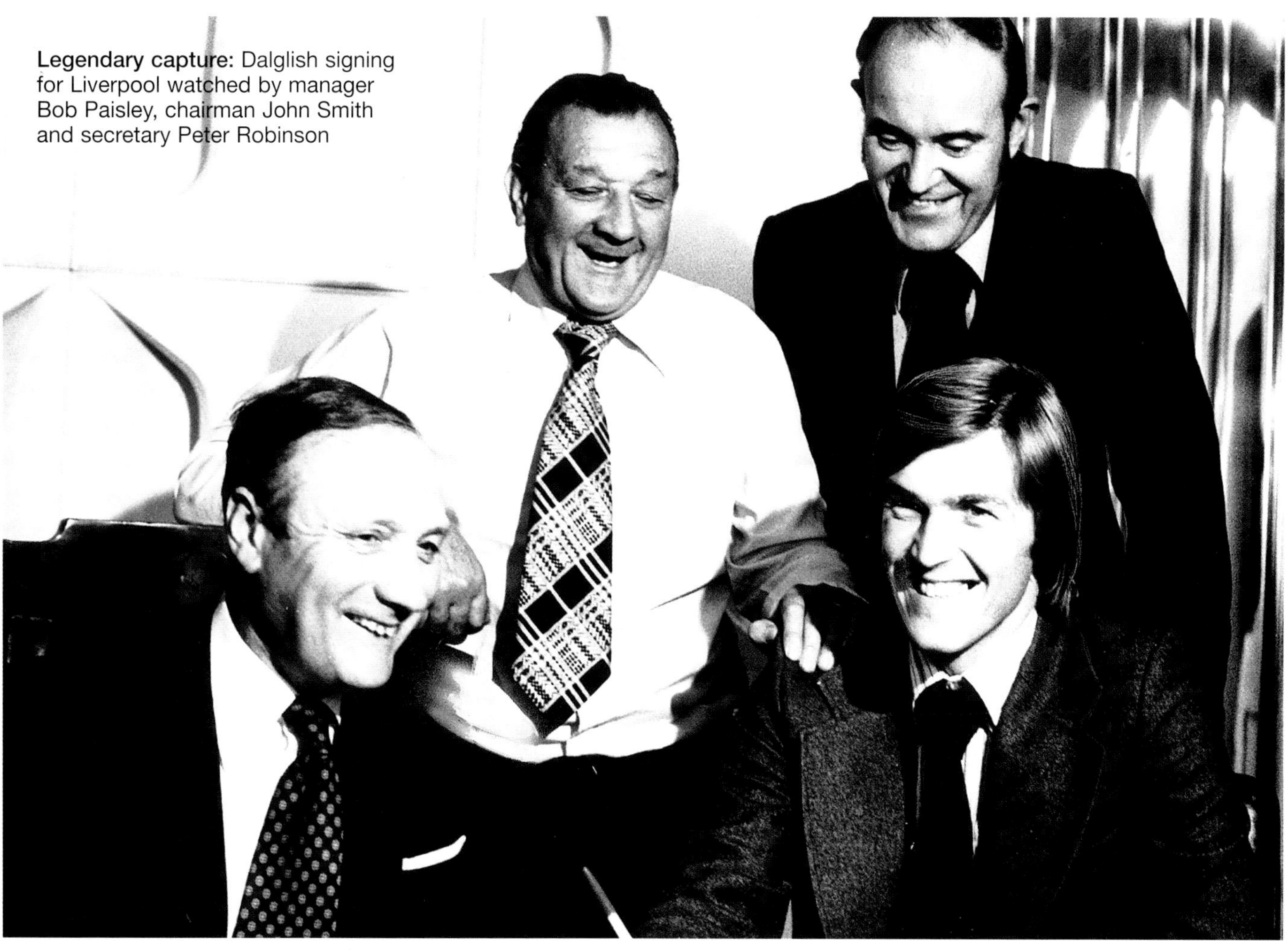

Legendary capture: Dalglish signing for Liverpool watched by manager Bob Paisley, chairman John Smith and secretary Peter Robinson

In the frame: Emlyn Hughes and Bob Paisley hold a portrait of the team in March 1979

Winning line-up: Terry McDermott, Emlyn Hughes, Phil Neal, Ray Kennedy, Phil Thompson and Ray Clemence

PAGE 30 DAILY MIRROR, Thursday, May 17, 1979

"Many sides will win the title. None will better us" — DON REVIE

FINAL TABLE IN 1968-69	P	W	D	L	F	A	Pts
Leeds ...	42	27	13	2	66	26	67
Liverpool	42	25	11	6	63	24	61

SUPERCHAMPS!

Paisley's pride go for record 68—at Leeds

By TONY STENSON

LIVERPOOL boss Bob Paisley (above) declared last night: "We intend to become Britain's greatest-ever team."

His incredible side stand on the threshold of smashing the all-time record of 67 points by a club winning the League championship—set by Don Revie's Leeds 10 years ago.

And tonight Leeds defend their place in football history. For if Liverpool, currently with 66 points, are to achieve their ambition they must do it at Elland Road.

Revie said after setting the record: "Many sides will win the title. None will better us."

But Revie obviously didn't know how great Liverpool were to become.

Any doubts that the Anfield giants might coast into their last game were dismissed by Paisley.

"There is still plenty to play for," he said.

"We're going for everything.

"A new points record would set the seal on a season when the players have done better than in any of the other championships I've been involved with."

Liverpool, champions four times since 1969, could establish two other records at Leeds.

They could let in five goals and still set an all-time record for the fewest goals conceded in a 42-match season.

And if they score twice they will cash-in on a £50,000 prize for hitting a target of 84 goals.

Ray Clemence, their England goalkeeper, could achieve the personal triumph of becoming the hardest man to beat in football. Clemence has let in only 16 goals in 41 league games this season—beating the old record of 24 he shares with his predecessor Tommy Lawrence and Nottingham Forest's Peter Shilton.

But all this leaves Leeds defender Paul Madeley unmoved. Madeley, 35, one of the two survivors of the record-breaking team, says:

"Teams here and at Liverpool have had one thing in common. We've been difficult to beat. I just wish we could have had Liverpool's continuity.

"But I still think the Leeds of 1969 were harder to beat than Liverpool are now.

"They can't touch our record of losing only two games ten years ago."

Leeds manager Jimmy Adamson has dropped England star Tony Currie for only the second time since his £245,000 move from Sheffield United in 1976.

This shock decision could mark the end of Currie's Leeds career.

TOP OF THE TABLE

	P	W	D	L	F	A	Pts
Liverpool	41	29	8	4	82	16	66
W B A	41	24	11	6	72	34	59
Nott'm Forest ...	41	20	18	3	60	26	58
Everton	42	17	17	8	52	40	51
Leeds	41	18	14	9	70	49	50

Keeper Ray Clemence . . . no sucker when the action starts.

RUGBY

ENGLAND'S RISING SONS SCORCH INTO EIGHTIES

From CHRIS LANDER In Fukuoka

THE England rugby team can lift their heads high again after a record-breaking 80—3 victory over Kyushu here yesterday.

In the wake of their traumatic two-points victory over Japan they blitzed the local province with 15 tries.

So confidence has been restored to Billy Beaumont's team by this record scoreline which easily eclipsed the previous best total of 64 points run up against Western Australia at Perth in 1975.

To give rugby fans at home some idea of the strength of Kyushu I would back them to hold their own against the best club and county sides in England.

England captain Beaumont agreed with my summing up when he commented: "I know people will see the scoreline and say the opposition must have been a lot of rubbish.

"Well tell them from me that they would be insulting Kyushu. I've played against far less accomplished footballing sides on major tours."

SCORERS.—KYUSHU: Pens: Takeshi, Nakamura. ENGLAND: Tries: Mike Slemen and John Scott (3 each), John Carleton, Nigel Pomphrey, Alastair Hignell (2 each), Richard Cardus, Ian Peck and Toby Allchurch. Cons: Huw Davies (10).

NON-LEAGUE

London clubs step into the 'big' time

BARNET, Gravesend, Maidstone and Wealdstone are the four London area clubs who have been selected for the non-league Premier Alliance, which starts next season.

Champions Worcester and Runners-up Kettering are also among the 13 Southern League clubs who will form the new league. The rest of the teams come from the Northern Premier.

The Alliance champions are to be automatically nominated for election to the Football League.

LEAGUE SCENE

NEW HOPE FOR PETCHEY'S MEN

MILLWALL go into tonight's match with Wrexham still hoping to make a sensational escape from relegation. George Petchey's men need to win their last two matches—both at the Den—by nine clear goals to stay in the Second Division, writes Kevin Moseley.

And they were heartened last night by the news that Wrexham have an injury crisis which leaves them without six first-team regulars.

Manager Arfon Griffiths will even be making a brief come-back at the age of 37.

Petchey said: "I still believe we have a chance."

FIXTURES

(7.30 unless state)

FIRST DIVISION
Leeds v Liverpool ....

SECOND DIVISION
Millwall v Wrexham ....

THIRD DIVISION
Shrewsbury v Exeter ....
Sheff. Wed. v Blackpool ....

FOURTH DIVISION
Hartlepool v Northampton (7.15) ...
Wimbledon v Darlington ....

Swindon fight—police may act in 48 hours

THIRD Division Swindon and Gillingham should hear in the next forty-eight hours if the police are to take action following an after-match fight earlier this month, writes Tony Stenson.

Swindon coach Wilf Tranter was injured in the players' tunnel after the promotion clash and a police spokesman said yesterday: "Our Chief Superintendent has all relevant reports and is now considering if court action should follow."

The FA are making their own inquiries.

Above: The Daily Mirror records Liverpool's latest title triumph and (below) setting a new Division One points record

Mirror Sport

Friday, May 18, 1979 No. 23,414
Telephone: (STD code 01)—353 0246
CHANNEL ISLANDS 9p

A frame-up as Faldo nicks a 65

NICK FALDO tamed the feared Old Course at St. Andrews yesterday with a record-equalling 65, to open up a three-shot lead on the first day of the £50,000 Colgate P G A championship.

And defending champion Faldo, who won by a massive seven-shot margin last year, said: "That's the most satisfying round I've ever played. "I'm going to frame that card and put it on the wall at home."

Faldo, Britain's most exciting prospect at 21, had switched back to the putter he used as an amateur in 1975. "It's the first time I've used it as a pro," he said.

"I felt a bid daft, changing the day before a big tournament. But I practised with both of them in my bedroom this morning and thought 'Oh hell, I'll give the old putter a try.' It was one of the best decisions I ever made."

It certainly was. He launched his birdie blitz by using the old putter to hole out from 35ft. at the first and an astonishing 30 yards at the fourth.

NICK FALDO

Liverpool prove they're super champs

RECORD BUSTERS

David Johnson hammers Liverpool's first goal.

It's glory all the way

By KEN REYNOLDS

LIVERPOOL walked alone into First Division history books at Leeds last night.

RESULTS AND SCORERS

FIRST DIVISION
LEEDS 0 LIVERPOOL 3

FIRST DIVISION

FINAL TABLE 1978/79

		Pld	W	D	L	F	A	GD	Pts
1	**Liverpool**	**42**	**30**	**8**	**4**	**85**	**16**	**69**	**68**
2	Nottingham Forest	42	21	18	3	61	26	35	60
3	West Bromwich Albion	42	24	11	7	72	35	37	59
4	Everton	42	17	17	8	52	40	12	51
5	Leeds United	42	18	14	10	70	52	18	50
6	Ipswich Town	42	20	9	13	63	49	14	49
7	Arsenal	42	17	14	11	61	48	13	48
8	Aston Villa	42	15	16	11	59	49	10	46
9	Manchester United	42	15	15	12	60	63	-3	45
10	Coventry City	42	14	16	12	58	68	-10	44
11	Tottenham Hotspur	42	13	15	14	48	61	-13	41
12	Middlesbrough	42	15	10	17	57	50	7	40
13	Bristol City	42	15	10	17	47	51	-4	40
14	Southampton	42	12	16	14	47	53	-6	40
15	Manchester City	42	13	13	16	58	56	2	39
16	Norwich City	42	7	23	12	51	57	-6	37
17	Bolton Wanderers	42	12	11	19	54	75	-21	35
18	Wolves	42	13	8	21	44	68	-24	34
19	Derby County	42	10	11	21	44	71	-27	31
20	Queens Park Rangers	42	6	13	23	45	73	-28	25
21	Birmingham City	42	6	10	26	37	64	-27	22
22	Chelsea	42	5	10	27	44	92	-48	20

A DECADE OF DOMINANCE

THE SUCCESS OF THE SEVENTIES ONLY WHETTED THE APPETITE FOR WHAT WAS TO BECOME THE GOLDEN ERA IN LIVERPOOL'S PROUD HISTORY. ASSURED OF THE STATUS OF ENGLISH FOOTBALL'S MOST SUCCESSFUL CLUB, A LEGION OF LEGENDS HELPED THE REDS TO A FURTHER SIX TITLES

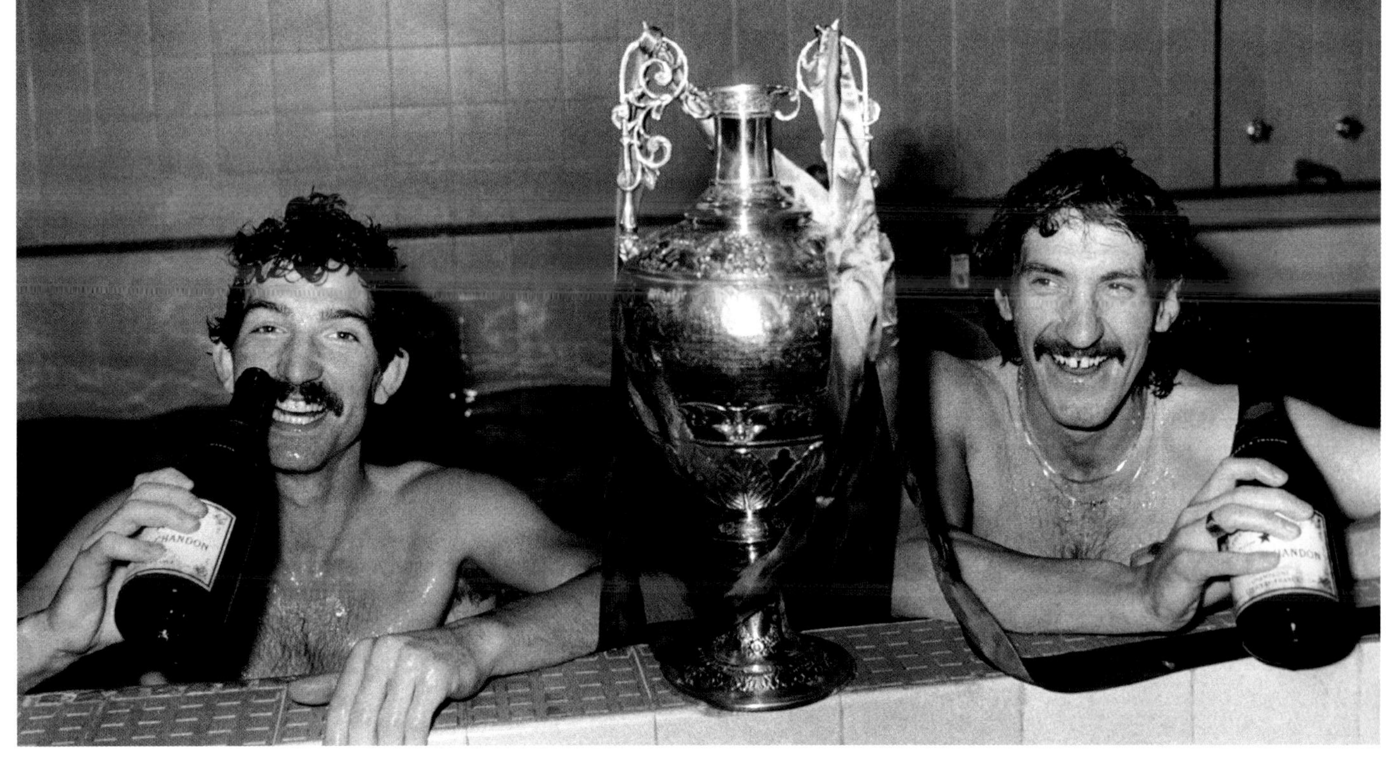

Bubbly bath: Graeme Souness and Terry McDermott enjoy some champagne after securing more league silverware

Mirror Sport

Saturday, May 3, 1980 (No. 23,770)

Manchester (STD code 061) 832-3444

CRUNCH DAY ON THE TITLE TIGHTROPE

Sexton 'going for broke'

By BOB RUSSELL

ROME AND DRY!

Italy repeat will clinch title—Paisley

By CHRIS JAMES

BOB PAISLEY last night sounded the call to arms for his weary battle-scarred troops to produce one more supreme effort in the push for the biggest domestic soccer prize of all.

The League title is all that remains for Liverpool after Arsenal shattered their double dreams with Thursday's FA Cup third replay defeat.

Midfield

Unchanged

Cast Iron's Wembley battle cry!

Picture: CHRIS PATERSON

ARTHUR BROOKS' RL FINAL FOCUS —Page 30

WE'RE GOING FOR KILL—WHITWORTH

By COLIN DIBALL

Positive

Pat on the back lifts Alex

SILVER DOLLAR only £16.95

UNITED STATES OF AMERICA

ONE DOLLAR

BLUEGROVE

FINAL TABLE 1979/80

		Pld	W	D	L	F	A	GD	Pts
1	**Liverpool**	**42**	**25**	**10**	**7**	**81**	**30**	**51**	**60**
2	Manchester United	42	24	10	8	65	35	30	58
3	Ipswich Town	42	22	9	11	68	39	29	53
4	Arsenal	42	18	16	8	52	36	16	52
5	Nottingham Forest	42	20	8	14	63	43	20	48
6	Wolves	42	19	9	14	58	47	11	47
7	Aston Villa	42	16	14	12	51	50	1	46
8	Southampton	42	18	9	15	65	53	12	45
9	Middlesbrough	42	16	12	14	50	44	6	44
10	West Bromwich Albion	42	11	19	12	54	50	4	41
11	Leeds United	42	13	14	15	46	50	-4	40
12	Norwich City	42	13	14	15	58	66	-8	40
13	Crystal Palace	42	12	16	14	41	50	-9	40
14	Tottenham Hotspur	42	15	10	17	52	62	-10	40
15	Coventry City	42	16	7	19	56	66	-10	39
16	Brighton & Hove Albion	42	11	15	16	47	57	-10	37
17	Manchester City	42	12	13	17	43	66	-23	37
18	Stoke City	42	13	10	19	44	58	-14	36
19	Everton	42	9	17	16	43	51	-8	35
20	Bristol City	42	9	13	20	37	66	-29	31
21	Derby County	42	11	8	23	47	67	-20	30
22	Bolton Wanderers	42	5	15	22	38	73	-35	25

Due a raise: Phil Thompson parades the championship trophy around Anfield after a 4-1 victory over Aston Villa in 1980

"Kevin was quicker off the mark, but Kenny runs the first five yards in his head"

– Bob Paisley

Great Scot: Kenny Dalglish is shadowed by fellow Scot Archie Gemmill as the Reds take on Birmingham City at St Andrews in September 1980

On their knees: Kevin Keegan's Southampton visit Anfield in February 1981 but were no match for a rearguard including Alan Kennedy and Alan Hansen as the Reds recorded a 2-0 win

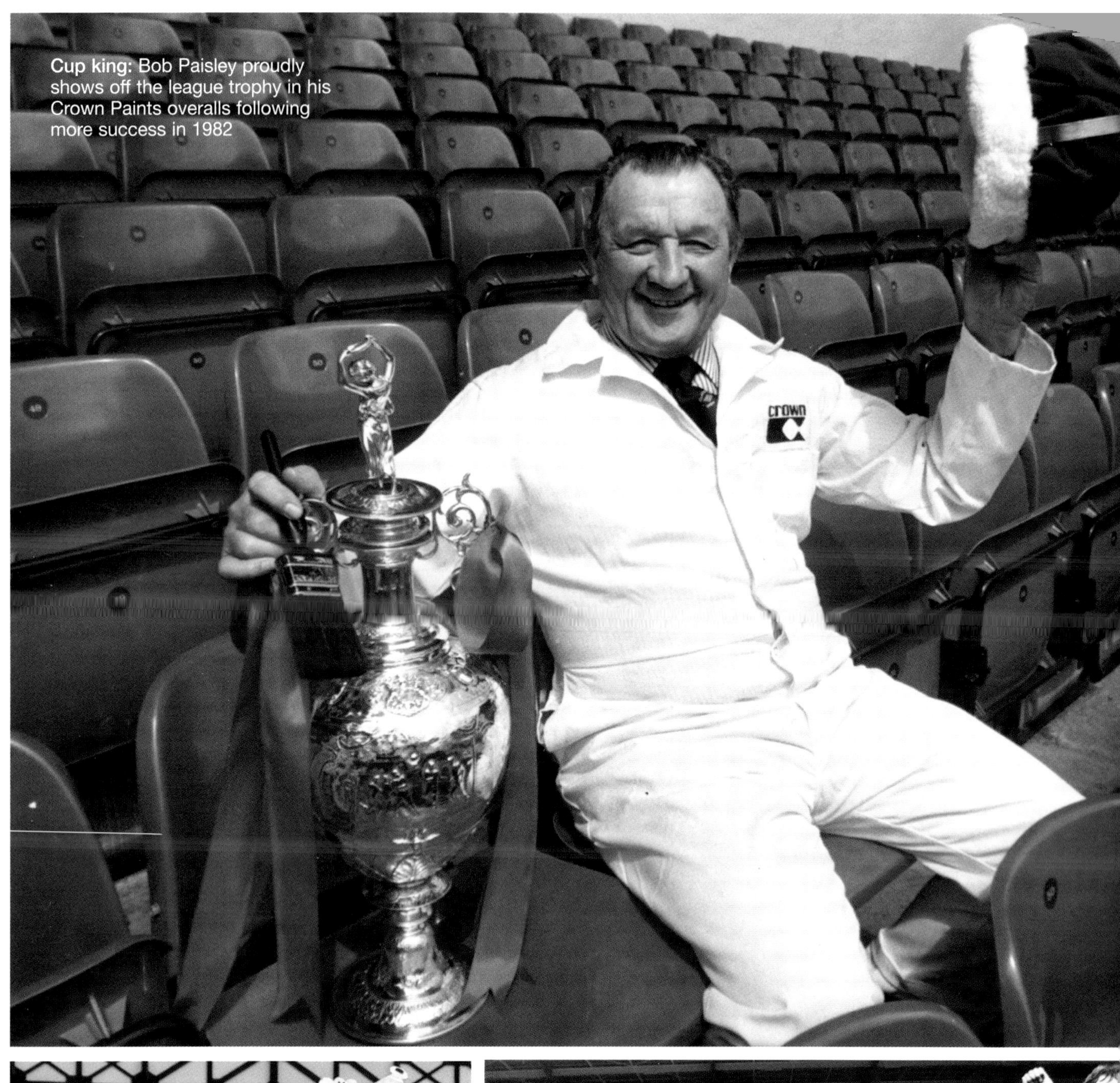

Cup king: Bob Paisley proudly shows off the league trophy in his Crown Paints overalls following more success in 1982

Fun and games: Bruce Grobbelaar tackles two pitch invaders at Goodison (left) and the 13th title celebrations get underway (right)

TOP OF THE FIRST

	P	W	D	L	F	A	Pts
Liverpool	41	26	8	7	80	32	86
Ipswich	41	25	5	11	73	52	80
Man. U.	42	22	12	8	59	29	78
Tottenham	41	20	11	10	66	48	71
Arsenal	42	20	11	11	48	37	71
Swansea	41	21	6	14	58	48	69
S'thampton	42	19	9	14	72	67	66
Everton	42	17	13	12	56	50	64
West Ham	42	14	16	12	66	57	58
Man. City	42	15	13	14	49	50	58

Quiet room at the top . . .

CHAMPAGNE and songs, laughter and congratulations provided all the joyous signs of Liverpool's 13th League championship in the dressing room, boot room, tea room and board room at Anfield after Saturday's 3-1 win over Tottenham had clinched the title.

There was only one quiet place in the building—the office of the administrative brain who runs the show, general secretary Peter Robinson.

And it was there that I had a privileged glimpse of the efficiency of the Liverpool system.

While other hands were reaching for bottles, Robinson's reached for the telephone. His first call, within minutes of the proud parade of the trophy around the ground, was to a hotel in Middlesbrough, cancelling a stay there by the team tonight for tomorrow's final match of a fabulous season.

"We would have felt it necessary to stay overnight if we still needed the points," said Peter. "Now we will travel up by coach and that will save around £300."

The money was put to immediate use. Peter's second telephone call was to the firm whose bulldozers moved in on Anfield yesterday to rip three inches off the pitch before work starts on re-laying it.

Liverpool's players have performed for the last time on a surface they have come to detest.

"It has been virtually unchanged for more than 50 years and has grown old and tired", says the groundsman who has just retired, 69-year-old Arthur Riley.

Liverpool's players and public will find that much has changed when they return to Anfield.

There will be seats on three sides of the ground, bringing an obvious increase in precious revenue—though no one would even contemplate the sacrilege of interfering with one of soccer's great institutions, The Kop.

PETER ROBINSON
Backroom genius .

What this confirms is that Liverpool do not merely move with the times. They set the pace, the example for the rest.

The changes in personnel this season have been well publicised. Top players have departed—Ray Clemence, Ray Kennedy, Jimmy Case, Avi Cohen, Colin Irwin.

Youngsters and new signings have taken their places—Bruce Grobbelaar, Mark Lawrenson, Ronnie Whelan, Ian Rush, Craig Johnston.

The paid professional staff has been reduced from 31 to 23

And huge salaries on long-term contracts may become a thing of the past, because Robinson estimates that Liverpool have suffered a reduction of 25 per cent in attendances over the last two seasons.

On Saturday when Liverpool went a shock goal down to Spurs after a glorious Glenn Hoddle strike that will abide in the memories of all those who saw it, it didn't seem to occur to them that there was any possibility of losing.

There was no fuss, no panic, no hurry, worry or fear. They continued to press, coldly and relentlessly, for victory.

It was fitting that two of the goals should come from the men manager Bob Paisley praised as the providers of the fresh legs and young spirits which revived Liverpool at Christmas, when they were stuck in 12th place—defender Lawrenson and the whispy Irish genius Whelan.

Hardest

Paisley, untypically, was almost eloquent afterwards when we had a quiet chat about his fifth championship in seven seasons.

"We brought in the fresh legs, not just because they were necessary, but because they were ready.

"There was no gamble, but it still made this the hardest championship we have won with me as manager."

It was equally fitting that Liverpool's most decisive goal—the one that put them into a 2-1 lead—came from that prince of players Kenny Dalglish.

I can think of few players in the British game, given so little time and room and facing a goalkeeper as accomplished as Clemence, who could have slotted a scoring shot with such chilling efficiency.

Liverpool's capture

JOHN McGREGOR, star amateur central defender with Scotland's Queen's Park, will sign for Liverpool today after rejecting a last-minute bid from Rangers.

Anfield favourite Ray Kennedy, who moved to Swansea in January, will share in Liverpool's League championship glory. He will get a winners' medal—a record sixth—because he played 14 games for Liverpool before his £160,000 transfer.

We are the champions . . . Kenny Dalglish (left) and captain Graham Souness show Liverpool's League championship trophy to the Anfield faithful.

Tosh is back in trouble

SWANSEA boss John Toshack is in trouble again with the Welsh FA after being booked for ungentlemanly conduct during his side's shock 2-1 home defeat to Middlesbrough.

Toshack, who was fined £200 only four months ago and £150 last season for bringing the game into disrepute, was cautioned by referee David Letts just before half-time. Earlier, Swansea's Ian Walsh had a goal disallowed and a penalty appeal was turned down.

"It was an embarrassing result for us and bad refereeing was partly to blame," said Toshack.

MANCHESTER CITY manager John Bond missed his side's 1-0 defeat at Sunderland to check on West Ham striker David Cross, while MANCHESTER UNITED'S teenage star Norman Whiteside scored a dream goal in the 2-0 home win over Stoke to earn a place on the club's Canadian tour.

HONEST CLOUGH SO HARD TO PLEASE

By JACK STEGGLES

Ipswich 1, Forest 3

PETER DAVENPORT earned rave reviews from Bobby Robson after blasting a hat-trick to finally torpedo Ipswich's championship challenge.

But there was no praise from his own manager Brian Clough.

"I signed Davenport from Cammell Laird in Birkenhead. And if he can't do better than that he'll be going back there," said Clough. "I know he scored three goals, but apart from that he did not play very well and I'm looking for more from him."

Clough said the same about Garry Birtles when he signed him from non-League Long Eaton. Birtles got a few goals for him—as well as more than £1 million when he sold him to Manchester United.

Davenport, a 21-year-old former Everton amateur brought his tally to four goals in the last two games—as many as £1 million striker Justin Fashanu has scored all season.

PETER DAVENPORT
. . .three not enough

"He was too quick and sharp for us and finished like a little wizard," said the admiring Robson.

Clough was also bitterly critical of Ipswich's decision to broadcast the fact that Tottenham had taken the lead at Liverpool over the tannoy system.

No doubt they hoped it would bring some urgency to a side playing from the start as if they knew the title was already beyond them.

"Ipswich were guilty of sharp practice there. I think it was disgraceful and am delighted it worked against them," stormed Clough.

Despite the bitter disappointment of finishing second yet again, Robson said: "We have still done well and people here have seen a ten-year miracle.

"We can be proud of running Liverpool so close on our limited resources. We can't match Liverpool for crowds or compete with them in transfer fees and wages. Yet we matched them most of the way in the title race—and that's a great achievement."

Alan Brazil was on the mark for Ipswich with his 27th goal of the season in answer to Davenport's trio.

First class for Ken

KEN BROWN . . couldn't believe it.

By TONY STENSON

Sheff Wed 2
Norwich 1

ON a day drenched in emotion, Norwich manager Ken Brown was the calmest of all.

He saw his brave Canaries lose their last match of the season, but Leicester's failure to defeat Shrewsbury ensured promotion to the First Division.

It was only later, when the singing stopped in the dressing room, that the stylish, elegant Brown let his mask slip.

"Of course it hurt when the critics had a go, but you just grit your teeth and carry on.

"But then someone said Leicester had only drawn. I just couldn't accept it and went looking for a television to find out if it was right.

Scene

There was a scene reminiscent of Villa's European cup semi-final with Anderlecht when Gary Bannister fired Wednesday's dramatic 89th-minute winner.

A fan was seen running around the goalmouth. "He was better placed than Bannister and deserved to be credited with an assist," joked Brown.

The goal signalled a mass invasion of the pitch where players were stripped almost naked by delirious fans.

A report of the incident is already on its way to the FA but from my point of view the invasion was just high spirits and not hooliganism.

Goal machine: Ian Rush fires a third past Leeds

FINAL TABLE 1981/82

		Pld	W	D	L	F	A	GD	Pts
1	**Liverpool**	**42**	**26**	**9**	**7**	**80**	**32**	**48**	**87**
2	Ipswich Town	42	26	5	11	75	53	22	83
3	Manchester United	42	22	12	8	59	29	30	78
4	Tottenham Hotspur	42	20	11	11	67	48	19	71
5	Arsenal	42	20	11	11	48	37	11	71
6	Swansea City	42	21	6	15	58	51	7	69
7	Southampton	42	19	9	14	72	67	5	66
8	Everton	42	17	13	12	56	50	6	64
9	West Ham United	42	14	16	12	66	57	9	58
10	Manchester City	42	15	13	14	49	50	-1	58
11	Aston Villa	42	15	12	15	55	53	2	57
12	Nottingham Forest	42	15	12	15	42	48	-6	57
13	Brighton & Hove Albion	42	13	13	16	43	52	-9	52
14	Coventry City	42	13	11	18	56	62	-6	50
15	Notts County	42	13	8	21	61	69	-8	47
16	Birmingham City	42	10	14	18	53	61	-8	44
17	West Bromwich Albion	42	11	11	20	46	57	-11	44
18	Stoke City	42	12	8	22	44	63	-19	44
19	Sunderland	42	11	11	20	38	58	-20	44
20	Leeds United	42	10	12	20	39	61	-22	42
21	Wolves	42	10	10	22	32	63	-31	40
22	Middlesbrough	42	8	15	19	34	52	-18	39

"I said that when I took over that I would settle for a drop of Bell's once a month, a big bottle at the end of the season and a ride round the city in an open top bus!"
– Bob Paisley

On target: Kenny Dalglish leaves Manchester United's Lou Macari and Gordon McQueen bemused

Jubilant: Bruce Grobbelaar struggles to contain his emotion

FINAL TABLE 1982/83

		Pld	W	D	L	F	A	GD	Pts
1	**Liverpool**	**42**	**24**	**10**	**8**	**87**	**37**	**50**	**82**
2	Watford	42	22	5	15	74	57	17	71
3	Manchester United	42	19	13	10	56	38	18	70
4	Tottenham Hotspur	42	20	9	13	65	50	15	69
5	Nottingham Forest	42	20	9	13	62	50	12	69
6	Aston Villa	42	21	5	16	62	50	12	68
7	Everton	42	18	10	14	66	48	18	64
8	West Ham United	42	20	4	18	68	62	6	64
9	Ipswich Town	42	15	13	14	64	50	14	58
10	Arsenal	42	16	10	16	58	56	2	58
11	West Brom	42	15	12	15	51	49	2	57
12	Southampton	42	15	12	15	54	58	-4	57
13	Stoke City	42	16	9	17	53	64	-11	57
14	Norwich City	42	14	12	16	52	58	-6	54
15	Notts County	42	15	7	20	55	71	-16	52
16	Sunderland	42	12	14	16	48	61	-13	50
17	Birmingham City	42	12	14	16	40	55	-15	50
18	Luton Town	42	12	13	17	65	84	-19	49
19	Coventry City	42	13	9	20	48	59	-11	48
20	Manchester City	42	13	8	21	47	70	-23	47
21	Swansea City	42	10	11	21	51	69	-18	41
22	Brighton & Hove Albion	42	9	13	20	38	68	-30	40

Nic of time: Steve Nicol scores his first goal for Liverpool, coming on as a 69th minute substitute for Craig Johnston and firing home the 83rd minute winner against QPR in October 1983

Golden Graeme: Graeme Souness takes on Watford's Kenny Jackett at Vicarage Road with title number 15 in sight

FINAL TABLE 1983/84

		Pld	W	D	L	F	A	GD	Pts
1	**Liverpool**	**42**	**22**	**14**	**6**	**73**	**32**	**41**	**80**
2	Southampton	42	22	11	9	66	38	28	77
3	Nottingham Forest	42	22	8	12	76	45	31	74
4	Manchester United	42	20	14	8	71	41	30	74
5	Queens Park Rangers	42	22	7	13	67	37	30	73
6	Arsenal	42	18	9	15	74	60	14	63
7	Everton	42	16	14	12	44	42	2	62
8	Tottenham Hotspur	42	17	10	15	64	65	-1	61
9	West Ham United	42	17	9	16	60	55	5	60
10	Aston Villa	42	17	9	16	59	61	-2	60
11	Watford	42	16	9	17	68	77	-9	57
12	Ipswich Town	42	15	8	19	55	57	-2	53
13	Sunderland	42	13	13	16	42	53	-11	52
14	Norwich City	42	12	15	15	48	49	-1	51
15	Leicester City	42	13	12	17	65	68	-3	51
16	Luton Town	42	14	9	19	53	66	-13	51
17	West Bromwich Albion	42	14	9	19	48	62	-14	51
18	Stoke City	42	13	11	18	44	63	-19	50
19	Coventry City	42	13	11	18	57	77	-20	50
20	Birmingham City	42	12	12	18	39	50	-11	48
21	Notts County	42	10	11	21	50	72	-22	41
22	Wolves	42	6	11	25	27	80	-53	29

Five star show: Ian Rush in his familar goalscoring pose as he puts five of six goals past hapless Luton in October

Sharp blunted: Bruce Grobbelaar saves a Graeme Sharp penalty as the Reds hold out for a 1-1 draw at Goodison Park in March '84 – a dress rehearsal for the League Cup final later that month

"It's best being a striker. If you miss five then score the winner, you're a hero. The goalkeeper can play a blinder, then let one in... and he's a villain"

– Ian Rush

Under control: Mark Lawrenson calmly ushers an Aston Villa effort just wide of the Liverpool goal during the closing stages of the '84/85 season in which the Reds finished second to derby rivals Everton. Ian Rush netted the winner, as he had done a week earlier when putting the fourth past Chelsea (top) in a 4-3 victory at Anfield

The King: Kenny Dalglish, now player-manager, fittingly scores the winner against Chelsea at Stamford Bridge to clinch the First Division title in 1986. He would later parade it alongside the FA Cup during the open-top bus tour around Liverpool (left), as he marked his first season in charge by completing the 'double'

FINAL TABLE 1985/86

		Pld	W	D	L	F	A	GD	Pts
1	**Liverpool**	**42**	**26**	**10**	**6**	**89**	**37**	**52**	**88**
2	Everton	42	26	8	8	87	41	46	86
3	West Ham United	42	26	6	10	74	40	34	84
4	Manchester United	42	22	10	10	70	36	34	76
5	Sheffield Wednesday	42	21	10	11	63	54	9	73
6	Chelsea	42	20	11	11	57	56	1	71
7	Arsenal	42	20	9	13	49	47	2	69
8	Nottingham Forest	42	19	11	12	69	53	16	68
9	Luton Town	42	18	12	12	61	44	17	66
10	Tottenham Hotspur	42	19	8	15	74	52	22	65
11	Newcastle United	42	17	12	13	67	72	-5	63
12	Watford	42	16	11	15	69	62	7	59
13	Queens Park Rangers	42	15	7	20	53	64	-11	52
14	Southampton	42	12	10	20	51	62	-11	46
15	Manchester City	42	11	12	19	43	57	-14	45
16	Aston Villa	42	10	14	18	51	67	-16	44
17	Coventry City	42	11	10	21	48	71	-23	43
18	Oxford United	42	10	12	20	62	80	-18	42
19	Leicester City	42	10	12	20	54	76	-22	42
20	Ipswich Town	42	11	8	23	32	55	-23	41
21	Birmingham City	42	8	5	29	30	73	-43	29
22	West Bromwich Albion	42	4	12	26	35	89	-54	24

crown paints
crown paints
crown paints
crown paints
crown paints
crown paints
crown paints
crown paints

PAGE 28 DAILY MIRROR, Monday, April 25, 1988 ★

SOCCER SPECIAL

Liverpool wra

WE'LL KOP

SMILE of a champion as Peter Beardsley celebrates Liverpool's 17th League title after scoring the winner against Spurs.
Pictures: ALBERT COOPER.

Lennie's laughing

By HARRY HARRIS Charlton 2, Newcastle 0

LENNIE LAWRENCE, the master of great escapes, is putting the relegation frighteners on London rivals Chelsea and West Ham.

The terrifying play-off position Lawrence describes from intimate knowledge as "traumatic and emotional" is set to face one of the three London clubs.

And Charlton are out to make sure it's not them, as the relegation finale reaches a climax.

Chelsea must go to West Ham and play Charlton at Stamford Bridge in the last game of the season.

Charlton's victory over Newcastle increased the tension at the bottom and Lawrence said: "For the last couple of matches we have hit top form, keeping six clean sheets in eight games — that's not bad by anybody's standards."

Optimism

Two early goals by Garth Crooks wiped out the Geordies and left Lawrence optimistic.

He said: "I've always said that 43 points will be enough — or 42 with a good goal difference.

"There's an outside chance Spurs could slip into the play-off dog-fight if they don't get a point at Luton. Otherwise it's between Derby, Chelsea, West Ham and us."

Mark blast

By IAN GIBB Oxford 1 Everton 1

OXFORD boss Mark Lawrenson hit out at the boo-boys who forced him to axe his keeper Peter Hucker.

Hucker was shattered by the decision, but Lawrenson said: "I had to leave him out because our fans slaughtered him in the last home game. It was diabolical."

Although the last rites still have to be read over Oxford's First Division life, Lawrenson is already laying his plans to bounce back next season.

By CHRIS JAMES
Liverpool 1, Tottenham

THE experts have argued for months ab... it . . . is this the greatest Liverpool te... of all time?

Now, as the Anfield kings celebrate yet other League title, we have the answer from the who should know — skipper Alan Hansen.

After the euphoria of Liverpool's champa party to celebrate their 17th League crown, Hansen admitted: "This could be the greatest team, but we're not there yet.

"We've done it in style this season, scoring lots of goals and not conceding many.

"But the Liverpool title-winning side of 1978-79 really turned on the style. That year we scored 85 goals and only let in 16 — and we played brilliant football.

"That was the great team. This one isn't there yet, but I'm convinced it will compare with them one day."

Hansen, who has now won seven championship medals, was a member of that superb 78-79 side which included s greats as Ray Clem Kenny Dalglish, Gra Souness and T McDermott.

Hansen underline belief that the pre Liverpool team are h ing for more glory he added: "I think team are going to from strength strength.

"Whether I'm a pa it remains to be I'll be out of the do soon as they think time is right becaus seen it happen t many players before

"It is the Liverpoo and I accept it. you've won somethi counts for nothin cause you're expect start again.

"That's what k you going more than thing here."

Liverpool, who ruled English socce quarter of a century have a thirst for which rema unquenched.

The Anfield stars

TOP OF THE TABLE

DIVISION 1

	P	W	F	A
Liverpool	36	25	79	20
Man Utd	36	19	61	35
Everton	37	19	51	24
Q.P.R	38	19	47	36
Nottm F	35	18	58	34
Arsenal	37	17	52	34
Wimbledon	36	13	55	44
Sheff W	37	15	47	57

LOYAL TONY

He backs Hammers

By JACK STEGGLES W Ham 1, Cov'try 1

TONY COTTEE still wants to leave West Ham, but not in the Second Division.

The little striker grabbed his first goal in 10 games to keep struggling Hammers out of the First Division play-off place.

Now he says: "In view of our crisis I have put off talks about my own future until the end of the season.

"But whether I stay or go I want West Ham to remain in the First Division. It would break my heart if they were relegated."

Mariner sinking

By GRAHAM BAKER Port'mth 2, Norwich 2

PAUL MARINER emerged from the fury of a last-minute penalty storm to admit that Portsmouth are sinking fast.

"It looks as if the penalty could decide our future with the other teams picking up points," said Mariner, adjudged to have handled after earlier putting Pompey 2-1 up.

Wayne Biggins netted the spot kick to push Pompey nearer relegation.

DAILY MIRROR, Monday, April 25, 1988 PAGE 29

p League title and say..

THE LOT!

This team will be the greatest

Kenny Dalglish opens the bubbly and allows himself a rare smile as he savours Liverpool's triumph.

Gordon puts a stop to the giggles

By NIGEL CLARKE: Wimbledon 2, Chelsea 2

JOHN FASHANU found out that Wimbledon have learned to live without him as they came close to humiliating a Chelsea side who were once again a massive disappointment.

The FA Cup finalists should have buried the Blues as they mixed their best football of the season with the customary physical edge

And said goal-scorer Lawrie Sanchez, who played superbly in midfield: "It's a fallacy that we are a one-man team.

"We were giggling among ourselves out on the pitch it was going so well. It was totally enjoyable.

"But at the end we were just sitting in the dressing room dazed because after being brilliant for 80 minutes we gave two goals away.

"Chelsea must be laughing their heads off. With that kind of good fortune they will definitely escape relegation."

Sanchez had put the Dons ahead and Dennis Wise, after seeing Kevin

COPPELL CHEER!

Plymouth 1, C.Palace 3

● CRYSTAL PALACE boss Steve Coppell took his side to the West Country two days early — and the move paid off with their first away win since Boxing Day.

● He opted against making the journey the day before the match saying: "We were beaten when we came here last season and this was a

SIZZLING GRAHAM

● GRAHAM GOOCH was again in blistering form for Essex yesterday as he hammered 90 off 87 balls to bring a nine-wicket win over Kent in the Refuge Assurance opening game.

● The previous day the England opener had hit a career-highest 275 against the same suffering attack.

● Hampshire's David Turner hit the day's only century — 103 not out — but his side were still beaten by Surrey by 22 runs.

Essex v Kent

CHELMSFORD.— Essex (4pts) won by 9 wkts.

KENT

Benson c East b Topley 9
Pienaar c East b Lever 6
Tavare b Miller 23
C Cowdrey c Lever b Miller 11
Hinks c Border b Topley 55
G Cowdrey b Gooch 45
Taylor c Border b Topley 7
Marsh c Fletcher b Pont 9
Ellison not out 14
Kelleher not out 7
Extras (b 1, lb 7, w 7) 15

Total (8 wkts — 40 overs) .201
Bowling: Lever 8-0-43-1; Pont 8-0-41-1; Topley 8-0-46-3; Miller 8-2-29-2; Gooch 8-1-34-1.

ESSEX

Gooch b Davis 90
Hardie not out 78
Border not out 26
Extras (lb 7, nb 1) 8

Total (1 wkt — 36.3overs) 202
Bowling: Kelleher 6-0-31-0; Ellison 8-0-40-0; Pienaar 4-0-23-0; Davis 7.3-1-41-1; C S Cowdrey 6-0-42-0; G R Cowdrey 5-0-18-0.

Hants v Surrey

SOUTHAMPTON.— Surrey (4pts) won by 22 runs.

SURREY

Richards c R Smith b Connor 30
D Smith lbw b Tremlett 75
Stewart c R Smith b James 53
Lynch run out 25
Ward c R Smith b Nicholas 8
Sadiq c Terry b Tremlett 0
Greig c James b Jefferies 5
Bullen c Nicholas b Tremlett 11
Feltham b Connor 18
Clarke not out 2
Peters not out 1
Extras (lb 7 w 1) 8

Total (9 wkts — 39 overs) .236
Bowling: Jefferies 8-2-26-1; Tremlett 7-0-48-3; Connor 7-0-40-2; James 8-0-46-1; Cowley 3-0-23-0; Nicholas 6-0-46-1.

HAMPSHIRE

R Smith c Bullen b Peters 6
Terry c Clarke b Feltham 43
Nicholas b Greig 2
Turner not out 103
C Smith c Ward b Bullen 10
Jefferies c Peters b Greig 39
Cowley not out 1
Extras (lb 10) 10

Total (5 wkts — 39 overs) .214
Bowling: Peters 8-1-22-1; Greig 8-0-27-2; Feltham 8-0-57-1; Bullen 8-0-51-1; Clarke 7-0-47-0.

Derbys v Leics

DERBY.— Derbys (4pts) won by 9 wkts.

LORY THIRST

e off their celebra- to set their sights rther glories.

ere is, of course, the matter of the FA Final at Wembley st Wimbledon in a or a unique second le in three years.

t Liverpool's vision pader than that.

ter Beardsley, with rd minute goal st Spurs worthy of a million British rec- player, clinched the and his first title l.

And he showed he has quickly acquired the Liverpool thirst for success.

"Now it would be nice to do the double and then go on one year to do a treble," he said.

"Liverpool have been so close so many times and I'd like to be a part of the team which does it."

Liverpool did, of course, add the European Cup to the League and Milk Cup double in 1984 to become the first English team to win three trophies in a season.

But Beardsley's eyes are on a clean sweep of the three major domestic honours.

He added: "I've got four more years here and I hope there'll be three or four more championships.

"I hope I can win a lot more, because that is why I came here.

"You hope to win the title in your first season. To win it with four games left is tremendous."

● THE true pe of Liverpool's champions will known until th allowed back in rope.

● Bob Paisley, t mer Liverpoo reckons it's imp to compare the c team with pre great sides beca the lack of in ment in Europe.

● He said: "I have liked t seen how they with the extra g

● "Another ei ten matche season might h ken the edg them."

FINAL TABLE 1987/88

		Pld	W	D	L	F	A	GD	Pts
1	**Liverpool**	**40**	**26**	**12**	**2**	**87**	**24**	**63**	**90**
2	Manchester United	40	23	12	5	71	38	33	81
3	Nottingham Forest	40	20	13	7	67	39	28	73
4	Everton	40	19	13	8	53	27	26	70
5	Queens Park Rangers	40	19	10	11	48	38	10	67
6	Arsenal	40	18	12	10	58	39	19	66
7	Wimbledon	40	14	15	11	58	47	11	57
8	Newcastle United	40	14	14	12	55	53	2	56
9	Luton Town	40	14	11	15	57	58	-1	53
10	Coventry City	40	13	14	13	46	53	-7	53
11	Sheffield Wednesday	40	15	8	17	52	66	-14	53
12	Southampton	40	12	14	14	49	53	-4	50
13	Tottenham Hotspur	40	12	11	17	38	48	-10	47
14	Norwich City	40	12	9	19	40	52	-12	45
15	Derby County	40	10	13	17	35	45	-10	43
16	West Ham United	40	9	15	16	40	52	-12	42
17	Charlton Athletic	40	9	15	16	38	52	-14	42
18	Chelsea	40	9	15	16	50	68	-18	42
19	Portsmouth	40	7	14	19	36	66	-30	35
20	Watford	40	7	11	22	27	51	-24	32
21	Oxford United	40	6	13	21	44	80	-36	31

So close: Ronnie Moran shouts instructions from the dug-out as Peter Beardsley races down the flank at Anfield. **Right:** John Barnes is consoled by Arsenal skipper Tony Adams after the Gunners pipped the Reds to the title on the final day of the 1988/89 season

THE LAST CHAMPIONS

LIVERPOOL'S DOMINANCE OF ENGLISH FOOTBALL APPEARED ENDLESS AS 11 LEAGUE TITLES WERE WON WITHIN 18 SEASONS. HOWEVER, 1989/90 PROVED TO BE THE END OF AN ERA – THE FINAL CHAMPIONSHIP FOR AT LEAST 20 YEARS AS A GREAT TEAM BEGAN TO BREAK UP

A familiar sight: Jan Molby and Gary Gillespie lead a lap of honour after the title was clinched against QPR in April 1990, while, left, Kenny Dalglish demonstrates his delight. At the top of the page, Glenn Hysen can be seen making his Liverpool debut in the 1989 Charity Shield

Wonder winger: John Barnes, the PFA Player of the Year, is seen getting the better of Aston Villa's Chris Price. Villa were the side who finished second in 1989/90

FINAL TABLE 1989/90

		Pld	W	D	L	F	A	GD	Pts
1	**Liverpool**	**38**	**23**	**10**	**5**	**78**	**37**	**41**	**79**
2	Aston Villa	38	21	7	10	57	38	19	70
3	Tottenham Hotspur	38	19	6	13	59	47	12	63
4	Arsenal	38	18	8	12	54	38	16	62
5	Chelsea	38	16	12	10	58	50	8	60
6	Everton	38	17	8	13	57	46	11	59
7	Southampton	38	15	10	13	71	63	8	55
8	Wimbledon	38	13	16	9	47	40	7	55
9	Nottingham Forest	38	15	9	14	55	47	8	54
10	Norwich City	38	13	14	11	44	42	2	53
11	Queens Park Rangers	38	13	11	14	45	44	1	50
12	Coventry City	38	14	7	17	39	59	-20	49
13	Manchester United	38	13	9	16	46	47	-1	48
14	Manchester City	38	12	12	14	43	52	-9	48
15	Crystal Palace	38	13	9	16	42	66	-24	48
16	Derby County	38	13	7	18	43	40	+3	46
17	Luton Town	38	10	13	15	43	57	-14	43
18	Sheffield Wednesday	38	11	10	17	35	51	-16	43
19	Charlton Athletic	38	7	9	22	31	57	-26	30
20	Millwall	38	5	11	22	39	65	-26	26

"Barnes did what we expected him to do. He made a goal, scored one, and entertained. You remember that"

– Kenny Dalglish

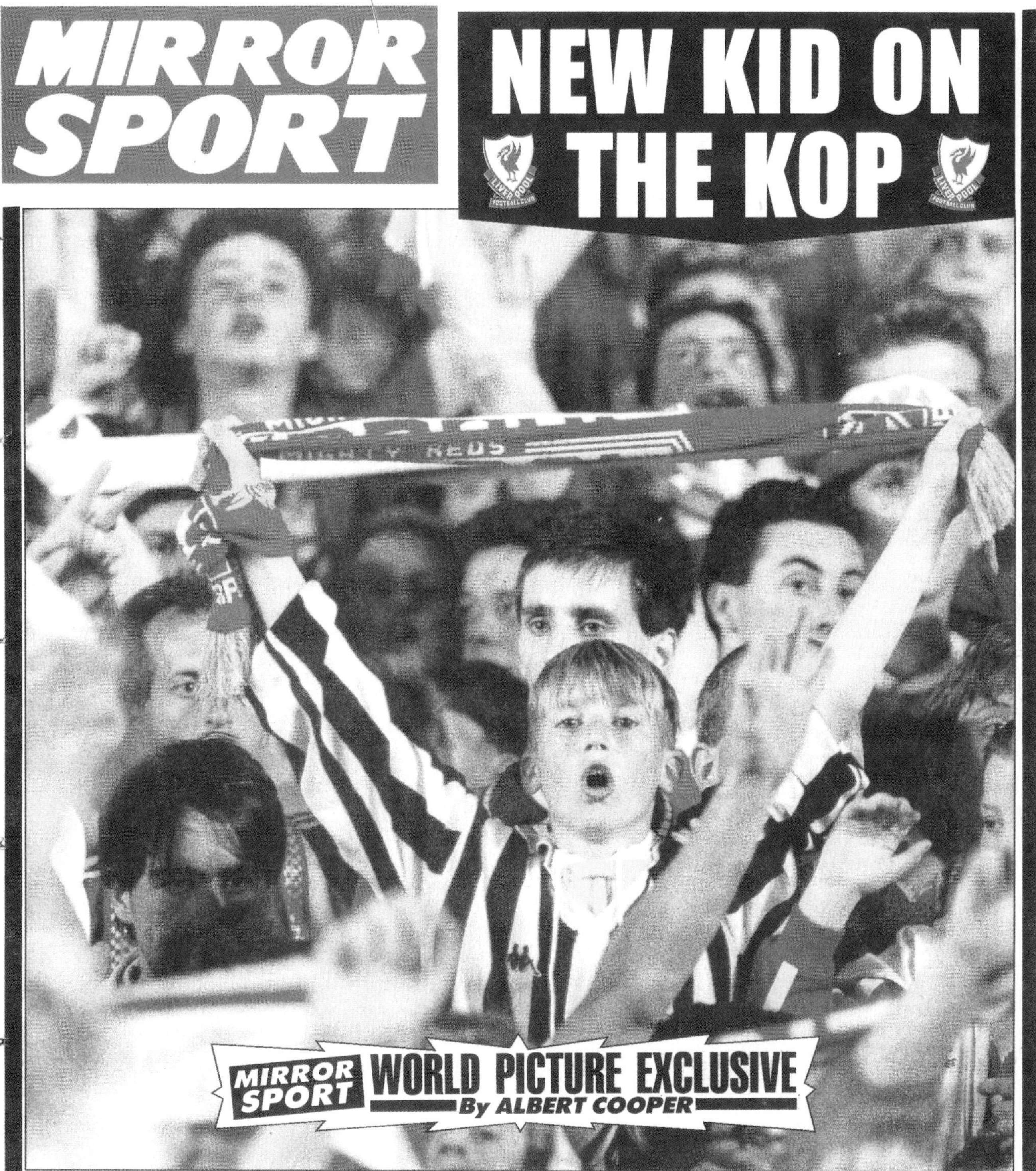

MIRROR SPORT

NEW KID ON THE KOP

KENNY'S No1 FAN

It's his son Paul aged 14

KOP this magic moment from a picture that says more than a thousand words.

By HARRY HARRIS

Kenny Dalglish's kid, Paul, the 14-year-old son of the Liverpool manager, is captured singing his heart out on the Kop.

It was on the night that his dad made a remarkable comeback at the age of 39 as Liverpool celebrated being crowned champions again.

Poignantly Kenny's boy was wearing a Juventus shirt, and such a fitting touch will not go unnoticed or unappreciated in Italy as English clubs are about to return to European competition six years after Heysel.

Mirror photographer Albert Copper freeze-framed one of the sporting moments of the new decade – the sheer exuberance of Dalglish's son, who was as proud as any of the Kopites belting out 'You'll Never Walk Alone' in appreciation of his dad's champions.

Young Dalglish saw what was probably the final appearance in the First Divison of his father, and what a moment it was as Liverpool celebrated their record 18th championship.

Daglish always insists that the players, the fans, and the management at Anfield are one big family, and this is why. There are few moments in sport as touching as this one.

Dalglish insists on keeping his family – four children and wife Marina – from the public gaze.

Kenny and his attractive wife emerged from their private world to comfort the bereaved families and the survivors of Hillsborough. They were commanding figures when Merseyside grieved.

But his children are rarely pictured in public. The last time I can recall was five years ago when little Paul was pictured with his big sister outside Buckingham Palace as Kenny received his OBE.

Dalglish raised his arms to salute the Kop after Liveprool's winner against Derby, and no one, apart from Kenny himself, knew that he as also saluting his son.

Who knows who was the prouder? Kenny at his boy Paul, or Paul at his father's achievements as Liverpool manager.

Published by Mirror Group Newspapers (1986) Ltd at 33 Holborn, London EC1P 1DQ (01-353 0246) and printed by Mirror Colour Print Ltd at Watford. Registered as a newspaper at the Post Office. Serial No. 27,069 ©The Daily Mirror Newspapers, Ltd., 1990 Thursday, May 3, 1990

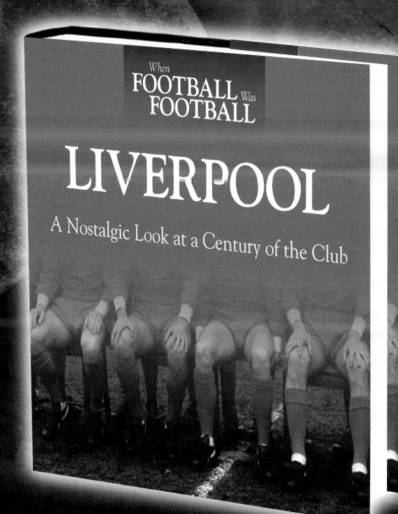

THE BARREN YEARS

THE FORMATION OF THE PREMIER LEAGUE BROUGHT ABOUT A SHIFT IN POWER. LIVERPOOL'S HALCYON DAYS OF LEAGUE DOMINANCE WAS REPLACED BY AN ERA WHERE MONEY RULED. ALTHOUGH THEY REMAINED COMPETITIVE, THE WAIT FOR TITLE NUMBER 19 CONTINUES

Behind enemy lines: Peter Beardsley fires home against Manchester United in September 1990

Flashback: Liverpool's squad of 1992 celebrate the club's centenary. They are, from left to right, back row: Jan Molby, John Barnes, Bruce Grobbelaar, Steve Nicol and Mark Wright. Front row: David Burrows, Ray Houghton, Ian Rush, Dean Saunders, Rob Jones and Ronnie Whelan

"You can't build a cathedral in a day. A look at the club's history tells you these things take time"

– Gerard Houllier

ENDING THE DROUGHT

AFTER DOMINATING ENGLISH FOOTBALL FOR SO LONG, IT'S HARD TO BELIEVE LIVERPOOL HAVE GONE ALMOST TWENTY YEARS WITHOUT A TITLE. HAVING FALLEN JUST SHORT IN LAST SEASON'S RACE, RAFA BENITEZ AND HIS MEN HAVE THE BELIEF THEY CAN FINALLY LAND NUMBER NINETEEN

New boy: Glen Johnson makes his Liverpool debut in a pre-season friendly against St Gallen

THE quest for 19 has been ongoing for 19 years and will have extended to two decades by next May. Will the holy grail be reached at that point?

When Alan Hansen lifted the league championship trophy in May 1990 nobody, surely, would have predicted the drought that was to come.

After all, Liverpool had won 11 titles in the previous 18 seasons and were firmly established as the dominant force in English football.

However, an era was ending. Kenny Dalglish made his final appearance when the trophy was awarded after a routine defeat of Derby, while Hansen had come off in the previous game because of a chronic knee injury that prevented him from wearing the red shirt again.

The likes of Steve McMahon, Ronnie Whelan and Steve Nicol had all reached their peaks. John Barnes still ran amok the following season but injuries would soon lessen his effectiveness.

Indeed, less than a year after the last title Dalglish would be gone altogether, resigning as manager as the pressures of the job post-Hillsborough took their toll.

His successors, Graeme Souness, Roy Evans, Gerard Houllier and, so far, Rafael Benitez have striven without success to take Liverpool back to the top, although there have been a few near misses along the way.

Last season they finished second with 86 points, four behind champions Manchester United. It was the highest Reds' total since the sublime 1987/88 title-winners ended a 40-game league campaign with 90 points.

Clearly they are not far away from reaching the summit but in 2008/09 there was something lacking that prevented them from overhauling Sir Alex Ferguson's team.

"We have to be strong next season. We have improved with Glen and hopefully we can do a little better and that will be enough"

– Rafael Benitez

Chelsea and United were both beaten home and away in the league, including the unforgettable 4-1 demolition at Old Trafford, so it's not results against their direct competitors.

What cost Liverpool was dropped points, especially at Anfield, against teams that should have been dismissed without too much fuss. Although they were unbeaten at home, seven matches ended in draws as the likes of Stoke, Hull, West Ham, Fulham and Manchester City shackled the Reds. United won 16 at home compared to Liverpool's 12.

There are few weaknesses in Benitez's team but the left side is definitely an area that could do with strengthening. Fabio Aurelio, Albert Riera and Ryan Babel are not players who the best sides eye with envy or cause much anxiety for those lower down the scale.

It's obvious but nonetheless true to say that the key men are Steven Gerrard and Fernando Torres, the world class spearhead of the Liverpool attack.

Injuries meant they only started together on 14 occasions in the Premier League last season. The Reds won 79% of those games. When either was missing, the win ratio dropped to 58%. These stark statistics tell you all you need to know about why Liverpool fell short. A world-class striker is a priority if the burden on Gerrard and Torres is to be eased.

At the time of writing, a worry was the future of Xabi Alonso, widely recognised among supporters as the player of the season in 2008/09. Alonso had handed in a written transfer request and if he were to depart, it would leave a significant hole in Benitez's preferred formation. So often the man who sets the tempo for Liverpool, controlling the game from in front of the defence, Alonso would not be easily replaced.

With two weeks to go before the league campaign began, the only major summer signing was Glen Johnson, recruited from Portsmouth for approximately £17m. Earmarked as Alvaro Arbeloa's replacement at right-back, his attacking intent gives him a versatility that means he can be effective in midfield. Towards the end of last season Johnson even made a couple of appearances stationed just off the Pompey strikers. He should prove a good acquisition.

So will this be the year for Liverpool? Time will tell but the reliance on Gerrard and Torres has to be a concern should a long-term injury afflict either of them. That said, Manchester United don't appear as formidable following the departures of Cristiano Ronaldo and Carlos Tevez.

The coming nine months should prove fascinating and thrilling viewing as the Reds seek to end that long, long wait. How sweet it would feel for the supporters if their team got to 19 first and re-established a league title lead over their great rivals.

FIXTURES 2009/10

AUGUST		
16	Tottenham Hotspur	A
19	**Stoke City**	**H**
24	**Aston Villa**	**H**
29	Bolton Wanderers	A
SEPTEMBER		
12	**Burnley**	**H**
19	West Ham United	A
26	**Hull City**	**H**
OCTOBER		
4	Chelsea	A
17	Sunderland	A
25	**Manchester United**	**H**
31	Fulham	A
NOVEMBER		
9	**Birmingham City**	**H**
21	**Manchester City**	**H**
29	Everton	A
DECEMBER		
5	Blackburn Rovers	A
12	**Arsenal**	**H**
16	**Wigan Athletic**	**H**
19	Portsmouth	A
26	**Wolves**	**H**
28	Aston Villa	A
JANUARY		
9	**Tottenham Hotspur**	**H**
16	Stoke City	A
26	Wolves	A
30	**Bolton Wanderers**	**H**
FEBRUARY		
6	**Everton**	**H**
9	Arsenal	A
20	Manchester City	A
27	**Blackburn Rovers**	**H**
MARCH		
6	Wigan Athletic	A
13	**Portsmouth**	**H**
20	Manchester United	A
27	**Sunderland**	**H**
APRIL		
3	Birmingham City	A
10	**Fulham**	**H**
17	**West Ham United**	**H**
24	Burnley	A
MAY		
1	**Chelsea**	**H**
9	Hull City	A

Attacking force: Fernando Torres gets a run out against a Thailand XI during the Reds' pre-season tour

LIVERPOOL SQUAD 2009/10

PLAYER	D.O.B	BIRTHPLACE
Goalkeepers		
Pepe Reina	31.08.82	Madrid (Spa)
Diego Cavalieri	01.12.82	Sao Paulo (Bra)
David Martin	22.01.86	Romford
Peter Gulacsi	06.05.90	Budapest (Hun)
Defenders		
Glen Johnson	23.08.84	Greenwich
Andrea Dossena	11.09.81	Lodi (Ita)
Daniel Agger	12.12.84	Hvidovre (Den)
Fabio Aurelio	24.09.79	Sao Carlos (Bra)
Emiliano Insua	07.01.89	Buenos Aires (Arg)
Jamie Carragher	28.01.78	Liverpool
Philipp Degen	05.02.83	Holstein (Swi)
Martin Skrtel	15.12.84	Handlova (Slo)
Stephen Darby	06.10.88	Liverpool
Martin Kelly	27.04.90	Bolton
Steven Irwin	29.09.90	Liverpool
Mikel San Jose	30.05.89	Pamplona (Spa)
Midfielders		
Steven Gerrard	30.05.80	Liverpool
Albert Riera	15.04.82	Manacor (Spa)
Xabi Alonso	25.11.81	Tolosa (Spa)
Yossi Benayoun	05.05.80	Dimona (Isr)
Javier Mascherano	08.06.84	San Lorenzo (Arg)
Lucas Leiva	09.01.87	Dourados (Bra)
Jay Spearing	25.11.88	Wirral
Damien Plessis	05.03.88	Neuville-aux-Bois (Fra)
Nabil El Zhar	27.08.86	Ales (Fra)
Forwards		
Fernando Torres	20.03.84	Madrid (Spa)
Andriy Voronin	21.07.79	Odessa (Ukr)
Dirk Kuyt	22.07.80	Katwijk (Hol)
Ryan Babel	19.12.86	Amsterdam (Hol)
David Ngog	01.04.89	Gennevilliers (Fra)
Krisztian Nemeth	05.01.89	Gyor (Hun)
Daniel Pacheco	05.01.91	Malaga (Spa)

* UP TO AND INCLUDING 31.07.09